United and Uniting

United and Uniting

An Ecumenical Ecclesiology for a Church in Crisis

ALBERT J. D. WALSH

WIPF & STOCK · Eugene, Oregon

UNITED AND UNITING
An Ecumenical Ecclesiology for a Church in Crisis

Copyright © Walsh 2011 Albert J. D. Walsh. Copyright © 2011 . All rights reserved. Except for brief quotations in critical publications or reviews, no part of this book may be reproduced in any manner without prior written permission from the publisher. Write: Permissions, Wipf and Stock Publishers, 199 W. 8th Ave., Suite 3, Eugene, OR 97401.

Wipf & Stock
An Imprint of Wipf and Stock Publishers
199 W. 8th Ave., Suite 3
Eugene, OR 97401
www.wipfandstock.com

ISBN 13: 978-1-61097-197-3
Manufactured in the U.S.A.

All scripture quotations, unless otherwise indicated, are taken from the Holy Bible, New International Version®, NIV®. Copyright ©1973, 1978, 1984 by Biblica, Inc.™ Used by permission of Zondervan. All rights reserved worldwide.

*For Kathlene
and the members of Heidelberg United Church of Christ.
Soli Deo gloria!*

Contents

Preface ix
Introduction xiii

1   The Issue 1

2   The Vital Importance of the Local Congregation 10

3   Ecumenicity and Conciliar Identity Formation 18

4   Autonomy in the Polity of the United Church of Christ 24

5   National Setting 32

6   Reflections: Pastoral and Theological 41

7   *Semper Reformanda* 49

8   *Place* as Metaphor: A Theological and Biblical Basis 63

9   Some Critical Observationss 72

10 The Contributions of L. Gregory Jones and George Lindbeck 83

11 Postscript 92

Bibliography 97

Preface

*Grace to you and peace from God
our Father and the Lord Jesus Christ.*

Rom 1:7

Thus the apostle Paul opens his letter to the church in Rome; a greeting familiar in the Pauline corpus, but one that is also of immense importance to the ecumenical ministries of the Church catholic.[1] The ecumenical ministry of the Church catholic could not exist were it not

---

1. Having looked for a definition of the term "Church catholic" (with an upper case "C") that would adequately convey my intent in its use, I found that while there were numerous definitions and/or descriptions that carried the weight of some of what I intend by the term, none was as graphic nor as profound as that found in the writing of Henri De Lubac. In his book *The Splendor of the Church*, De Lubac speaks of the Church catholic in this way: "The Church . . . is not God, but she is 'the Church of God'. She is His inseparable Bride, serving Him in faith and justice; she is the House of God and it is in her that He welcomes us to forgiveness of our sins. It is in this Church, 'the pillar and firmament of truth', that we believe in Him correctly, and glorify Him. . . . It is the place chosen by God for the invocation of His name, the temple in which we worship the Trinity and . . . 'the unshakeable sanctuary outside which, save with the excuse of invincible ignorance, we cannot hope for salvation' . . . she is the dwelling-place prepared on the mountain-tops and foretold by the Prophets, to which, one day, all nations are to come to live in unity under the law of the one God. She is the treasure-chamber in which the Apostles have laid up the truth, which is Christ; the one and only hall in which the Father celebrates the wedding of His Son; and since it is in her that we receive forgiveness, it is through her that we have access to life and the gifts of the Holy Spirit. We cannot believe in her as we believe in the Author of our salvation, but we do believe that she is the Mother who brings us our regeneration." De Lubac, *Splendor of the Church*, 19–20.

I contend that the reality or actuality of this descriptive of the "Church catholic" (with an upper case "C") *subsists* (with apologies to my Roman Catholic brethren should this use be offensive to their ecclesial sensibilities!) within the local congregation and wider "church" ("church" with a lower case "c") but always and everywhere with evidence of sin and human error. Rather than employ the language of "visible" and "invisible," I much prefer the Mercersburg delineation of "ideal" and "actual" Church (see Littlejohn, *Mercersburg Theology*, 66–83).

for the continuing presence, or I should say "gift" of both *grace* and *peace*. From the outset: nothing of any lasting value, nothing beyond that which is purely superficial, has been, can be, or will ever be accomplished in the Church catholic, or with the ecumenical movement itself, that hasn't been funded by God's grace! Grace is the first and last word in the lexicon of faith as it is in the ministry and mission of ecumenicity. Grace is made manifest, supremely, in Christ Jesus and only secondarily in and through the mission and ministries of the Church catholic.

The Greek word here translated as "peace" (*eiréne*) is the basis of our English term "irenic," which connotes more than peace as the absence of conflict. To have an irenic spirit is to be driven by the desire to achieve a viable reconciliation, seeking commonalities without ignoring or dumbing down those differences that once brought about separation from the other or others. The Greek term resonates at its deepest levels with the Hebrew *shalom*, as the promise of and petition for that peace evident in the rest of the Sabbath, which is a foretaste of the coming reign of God in which *shalom, peace*, will prevail throughout. It is the consummated unity of God's coming kingdom, revealed in the person, message, and ministry of Jesus and foreshadowed in the Church catholic, which is the driving engine of each and every effort of our ecumenical concern and conciliatory conversation in the church.

To have an irenic spirit is to enter into dialog from within an appreciation for one's own received biblical and theological tradition, yet with an openness to learn and receive gratefully from the biblical, theological, and historical certainties of one's partner in dialog. To have an irenic spirit is to stand on the firm foundation of one's faith convictions and yet remain attentive to the shifting winds of the Holy Spirit; it is to embrace a form of vulnerability that waits, in prayerful silence, for the spiritual awakenings and insights that come as a gift, and by grace alone. While ecumenical conversations continue at the level of national and global endeavor, there is now a need for the grassroots to be educated and immediately engaged in those same ecumenical endeavors, and perhaps even explore new and Spirit-driven approaches to conciliation, and in particular in any body of believers who, like the United Church of Christ, define themselves as a *united* and *uniting* church.

When I entered into the research for this book, which was at the time the groundwork for my doctor of ministry thesis,[2] I became increas-

---

2. Published under the original title of the doctoral thesis: *Learning the Grammar*

ingly alarmed to note how far my own confessional community (United Church of Christ) had drifted from the original ecumenical vision that served as the nexus of her birth. The UCC is not the only mainline denomination in the United States to have all but abandoned the theological traditions of Western Christianity, and in particular those disclosing the unity we share in Christ with other confessional communities. Yet because this has been my own community of faith for more than thirty years, I can only speak from within this particular experiential context. Even so, I would hope that what I have to offer would be of value to members of confessional communities other than the United Church of Christ. In fact, I would be even more bold and assert that the argument of this book is relevant to all Christian communities, as we are all each of us under the same mandate of Christ's high priestly prayer in John 17 and cannot escape accountability for the demise of efforts to bring about greater visibility of the oneness we share in Christ Jesus!

---

of an Ecumenical Faith: Education and the Formation of Conciliar Identity in the Local Congregation (Saarbrucken, Germany: VDM Verlag Dr. Muller Aktiengesellschaft & Co. KG, 2009).

Introduction

If we had our way, we would prefer to keep detouring around the decisions confronting us. If we had our way, we would prefer not to be dragged into this fight over the church. . . . But—God be thanked—it is not up to us. With God, we get just what we don't want. . . . We will not be spared any of this—making a decision means that we differ with others.

BONHOEFFER, BERLIN: 1932–1933

THE WORDS ARE THOSE of Dietrich Bonhoeffer taken from a sermon based on the text of Matt 16:13–18 regarding the "rock" upon which Christ said he would one day build his church. These words were spoken with courage in a time when the church in Germany was under assault from both the Nazi Party and those called "German Christians." All who are familiar with the struggles of the Confessing Church, and the efforts of those who, like Pastor Bonhoeffer, protested the misappropriation of the Old and New Testaments—as well as a contamination of the church and her ministry by a malevolent political machine—know only too well the seriousness and urgency of the crisis that these valiant souls faced with the danger of imprisonment and the specter of death crouching at their door. Even so, they stood their ground in an unrelenting effort to preserve the message, ministry, and mission of the church from the machinations of those who sought only to use and abuse the same for corrupt, even criminal, personal and political ends.

There were those in this same struggle who claimed the church in Germany was in peril of such temptation long before the Nazi Party took power, mostly as a consequence of the liberalization of biblical and theological doctrines in the life of the church, and in particular in those academic centers responsible for the education and training of candidates for pastoral ministry. It was in many ways the same enemy at which Karl Barth had first taken aim in his commentary on Romans; the perceived adversary was a form of hermeneutic that allowed little room for the influence of doctrinal assertions once considered the bedrock of confessional Christianity, an intolerant position that no longer saw value in such ancient doctrinal declarations.

While I am in no position to assert that we presently find ourselves in a situation of crisis as dire as that of Pastor Bonhoeffer and his contemporaries, I do contend that we face a crisis in the present-day church that is for our own time and in its own way of equal urgency.[1] We in the United Church of Christ have been lulled into a sense of complacency while our church has drifted further and further from the covenanted purpose (what I will call throughout this work her vision-and-vocation[2]), which was affirmed at her birth and essential to the formation and content of her identity from the beginning; I'm referring, precisely, to her *ecumenical* character. Moreover, I would affirm that there has been and continues to be a crisis in what was once called the *ecumenical movement*, which in many ways runs parallel to a similar crisis that has evolved historically in the United Church of Christ.

---

1. In R. R. Reno's disturbing and challenging book, *In the Ruins of the Church: Sustaining Faith in an Age of Diminished Christianity*, he speaks of the contemporary church in language reminiscent of the fall of Jerusalem prior to the Babylonian exile, so that the church "in ruins" becomes his prevailing metaphor and the basis for his constructive proposal. As an Anglican theologian, Reno offers profound insights concerning the "debilitation of Christianity" within his own confessional body with applicability to other Protestant denominations as well. I would not hesitate to borrow that same metaphor (i.e., "ruins") for what I perceive to be the current crisis in my own confessional community (the United Church of Christ). See R. R. Reno, *In the Ruins of the Church*.

2. By each use of the term "vision-and-vocation," I intend to speak of a reality whose origin is in God and granted by God as the continuing gift of the Holy Spirit. The term "vision" refers to that which God alone has provided this conciliar fellowship—an insightful, motivational perception—and discernment of the oneness (unity) God desires for the Church, and the wisdom which would accompany such a God-given and sustained vision shared with the wider church. By "vocation" I mean to imply a reality that presses far beyond what we would normally associate with the term, as in some profession or other chosen by an individual which only subsequently becomes a "way of life." I use the term "vocation" to refer to the call of God, a call to this conciliar fellowship in particular, whose identity as a Christian body and whose "form of life" is to be shaped by such "vocation." Without attendance to the "vision," the "vocation" will suffer impoverishment; without participation in and fulfillment of the "vocation," the "vision" will be diminished. The "glory" of the UCC is most fully evident in this, her faithful engagement with the "vision-and-vocation," which sets her apart from those bodies (and in particular in Protestant traditions) who would define themselves primarily by use of denominational traits and characteristics.

Introduction xv

While I address myself to the United Church of Christ in particular throughout this book, I believe the essential matter of both my contention and proposed conclusion is applicable to other confessional communities as well, and in particular those that have had an investment in the movement itself. While my experience has been within the boundaries of the church in its North American setting, I contend that the argument made and assessment given is likewise applicable to churches of the Western tradition far more than it is those of the Eastern and Pan-Orthodox.

After thirty years in ordained ministry in the United Church of Christ, having served the entire time in the pastoral office of the local congregation, I feel as though the following analogy best describes my growing sense of both distress and expectation. I am standing at the edge of a huge length of water, with an expansive bridge, still under construction, spanning half the distance between me and the far horizon. Having received communiqués from those who are residing on that same farther shore, I am painfully aware of two things: they are my extended family and dearest friends, and the distance between us has remained in its present condition for far too long. From both sides we wonder why the construction has ceased, and why the only activity on the bridge appears to have been cosmetic, little more than attempts to paint the pylons or service the existing support cables. When and why was the hard labor of a constructive effort discontinued?

The book you hold in your hands was not written as sharp criticism of those who have given so much to the ecumenical endeavors of the last fifty years, nor is it intended to chastise the leadership of my own confessional community, colleagues, or national staff. It is that I have finally come to a place where I must write what I hope will be a constructive contribution to a conversation concerning recommended ways in which we can once again attend to the construction of the bridge the Lord has committed to the care of all people. I am absolutely convinced that we will never achieve the purposes for which Christ brought *this* confessional community (i.e., UCC) into historical existence until we return to the fundamental faith of our founders, which was and remains essentially *ecumenical*.

Using the language of Pastor Bonhoeffer, I believe we are being summoned to a time of *decision*, to face the present crisis of the church with the courage of those convictions that have sustained Christ's *com-*

munio sanctorum for more than two thousand years,[3] or as some have said and more eloquently, a return to those faith convictions and doctrinal affirmations that were once considered inviolable and essential as representative of unity in Christ Jesus. We will not achieve the supreme purposes for which we were given birth as a confessional community with tricky quotes from TV or Hollywood comedians (i.e., the "God is still speaking" campaign), nor will we demonstrate to the wider church our faithful resolve to be a *united* and *uniting* church by advocating a contemporary form of biblical fundamentalism (i.e., "Biblical Witness"). There is more immediate to us the glorious vision and exceptional venture of those "guiding lights" who came together under the prayerful direction of the Holy Spirit to seek a more visible unity among Christians of diverse confessional commitments, historical heritage, and liturgical styles.

I would not want to appear insensitive to the plaintive cries of those from any number of societal groups calling for greater justice; I have no argument with the church tackling some of the most controversial social and political issues of our time. But I am deeply concerned that the prevalence of terms like "lesbian, gay, bisexual, transgender, transsexual," and others have come to dominate the focus of the church, even though such language has no place in the lexicon of any one confessional community! The language we use and the manner in which we use such language—as well as the priority given to its use—does suggest that *these* are the critical, if not central concerns with which the church must deal immediately and extensively. I would argue that we do not bring "justice" to any form of injustice simply by making room (i.e., becoming "Open and Affirming") in the pew for those persons experiencing such "injustice," any more than I can claim to be a crow by virtue of the fact that I have placed a black feather in my cap! When a church has covenanted to carry forward so mammoth a task as seeking to pursue and promote ever greater forms of visible unity among Christians of diverse

---

3. Josef Jungmann defines the term *communio sanctorum* as expressing "the fact that the Church is a holy community—a community created through the action of the Holy Spirit, who breathes a soul into the church, nourished through the sacraments, in particular the Eucharist. Therefore, the phrase *communio sanctorum* expresses a bond and communion among members of a living body. . . . In patristic literature, the *communio sanctorum* indicated . . . a community which was one in that it shared the same faith, the same hope, the same sacraments, the same pilgrimage and goal." Jungmann, "The Holy Church," 32–33.

traditions, it is unseemly to suggest that this is now merely one of several priorities—and no longer holds the capital claim to our energy, enthusiasm, creativity, prayer, and practice.

We need not, and in fact cannot, merely replicate the voices nor revamp the vision of those who gave so faithfully to the formation of this church; we can, however, commit ourselves to the retrieval of the fundamental features of *ecumenicity* that were once the heart and soul of the wider church's self-understanding and self-identity. To that degree, I argue one's identity as a conciliar Christian is based on appreciation for, and an awareness as well as internalization of, the biblical, theological, historical, creedal, and confessional elements that have always been essential to the self-understanding of the Church catholic, as the heart and soul of the ecumenical endeavor.

Here is my major thesis: The United Church of Christ was born of the mediation and guidance of the Holy Spirit to be first and foremost a bulwark in the often tangled but nonetheless breathtaking task of ecumenicity; this was her God-given vision-and-vocation. Therefore the identity and self-understanding of this conciliar fellowship is Christ centered and ecumenical in nature; membership in this confessional body is fundamentally conciliar; a Christ-centered ecumenicity must shape, inform, and characterize the whole of our ecclesiology as can nothing else of any theological merit.

This is the touchstone to which we must return again and again if we are to avoid any further drift into a series of experimentations with identities that are, perhaps, a genuine effort to address contemporary culture, yet are at risk of betraying the fundamental identity and consequent purpose for which our confessional community came into being.

Any ecclesiology—even one founded on fine theological principles—other than *ecumenicity* will ultimately prove fruitless and merely drain the church of energy and resources; this is not only a probable troubling reality but one that has been substantiated by the history of the United Church of Christ over the last three decades. At its most basic level, the Greek *ecclesia* means "a people called forth"; it is the affirmation of the reality of the church as a body brought into existence not so much (if at all!) of its own effort or energy, but more so, in language borrowed from John's Gospel, "born, not of the blood or of the will of the flesh or of the will of man, but of God" (John 1:13). "Born," of course, to a particular purpose, "called forth" from the world to serve the world in obedience to him who commands love; the church can only embody the Church catholic in obedience, worship, fellowship, and compassionate service, proclaiming a gospel of grace and forgiveness in a world that persists in forgetting both its origin and its end (*telos*) in God and therefore its accountability to God.

The ontological reality of the Church catholic is, in fact, a *given* under the gracious merits of Christ Jesus, the deliberate intentions and intercessions of the Holy Spirit, and as fulfillment, in part, of the providential plan of God the Father. As a "people called forth" the Church catholic exists *in* the world (though not *of* the world) as a *communio sanctorum* bearing testimony to the continuing presence of Christ with and within the church, for the world. All other ministries originate in the church's self-understanding (i.e., ecclesiological conceptualization) and are shaped by both the form and content of her ecclesiology. Please note, I said "ministries," not doctrinal or dogmatic declarations; what I mean to say is that the manner in which we understand who we are in Christ, and as the embodiment of Church catholic, will profile the characteristics and content of how we do ministry as church within and for the world, to the glory of God.

While the Church catholic has the undeniable component of humanity, with all the complexity and inconsistency one associates with being human evident throughout, she has not been given over (some might say "handed over"!) to the complete control of humans; i.e., she is the "body" that is under the authority of and accountable to the "Head"! It is just *this* truth which I fear is so often forgotten, or perhaps even denied, in the church today; many seem to be under the misconception that the church exists to serve the "felt needs" of her members and is best served when she conforms to corporate models of management rather than to the biblical and theological realities that have sustained her life for more than two thousand years.[4]

---

4. Even though De Lubac references the relationship between "church and state" in the following quote, I assert that his observation and implicit warning bear decisively on what I perceive to be the prevailing tendency (or should we say "temptation") of the United Church of Christ to a flirtation with "the world," as manifest in the form of contemporary culture with its own "godless" agenda: "Every form of separation and union of the two has its own dangers, and the symbioses of the greatest perfection are by that very fact the more dangerous, for here the best runs easily into the worst, and when it does it is not always clear which power has become the slave of the other—whether it is the Church which is dominating over 'the world,' or the world which is taking possession of the Church." De Lubac, *Splendor of the Church*, 115.

Even those forms of spirituality that once nurtured the church's sense of connectedness to Christ as Head have been given over to a managerial style so that prayer becomes just another attempt to control the direction we have already agreed the church should take, the mission she should undertake, or the way in which she should structure her ministries. God is simply called in to approve and consecrate decisions already predetermined in advance of prayer!

Our proposed ecclesiology is, therefore, far more than fine tuning of our theological conviction concerning who we see ourselves to be as church. *Ecclesiology* is fundamental to every other aspect of the church as *church* and to the ministries she will undertake in the name of Christ, as a "people called forth," and to the glory of God. If we embrace a definition of the United Church of Christ as fundamentally *ecumenical*, we are, and at the same time, determining both the shape and content of the *ecclesiology* that we will affirm as essential to our self-understanding and identity as church in a fragmented and disharmonious world.

Self-preservation is not a virtue to be encouraged as a motivational force in the life of Christ's *ecclesia*; self-preservation cannot be said to constitute a valid reason for the development of ministries intended to attract those who presently remain outside the boundaries of the church in order to gain on sagging membership rolls, and yet to listen to many members and leaders at the level of the local congregation, one would think membership decline and self-preservation were the most important issues facing the church. This same concept of self-preservation is evident throughout every stage of the organizational structure of the United Church of Christ, at the local, association, conference, and national levels as well.

There are often comparisons made between the "old-line" or "mainline" denominational churches and those often referred to as "mega" or "new paradigm" churches. One is left to wonder how any comparison can be made between these two very different forms of being church, and in particular when so many of the latter seldom make use of the term "church" in self-referential materials or even on their sign boards (for example, often such churches go by names like "family fellowship" or "faith community"). How one is to understand this phenomenon of the last four decades is a topic for another day; I merely want to assert that the effort to understand just how and why we are church cannot be accomplished through any such comparisons, just as the fundamental reason for the church's existence must be far more than mere self-preservation.

It cannot be denied that for at least the last three decades most mainline churches have been hemorrhaging members at an alarming rate and that this is a serious issue demanding approaches based on greater biblical and theological study and reflection than has been evident to date. Yet I contend that the most critical issue facing the church today is the question of identity and self-understanding in light of the substantive traditions, confessions, and doctrinal affirmations of the past; in particular, for the United Church of Christ, it is the question of identity in light of those traditions of biblical and theological conviction located in the rich *ecumenical* heritage of her vision-and-vocation.

For all intents and purposes, our church has now replaced the key symbol of our ecumenical community (the Cross of Victory or the Cross Triumphant) with a comma, and that as a consequence of a comedic comment attributed to the late Gracie Allen ("Never place a period where God has placed a comma"). Simply adding the theological subtlety "God is still speaking" does not make this commercial and solely promotional enterprise any less outrageous. Are we then to assume that there was absolutely *nothing* in the magnificent ecumenical heritage of the church that would have proven more transparent of our unique identity, more faithful to our vocation and more fruitful as an expression of a vision yearning to be further realized and awaiting fulfillment in God's future and in God's time?

I acknowledge that there are moments in the commercials associated with this promotional pitch that give personal testimony to the *ecumenical* character of our church, but seldom if ever is ecumenicity the core characteristic in the projected image of who we are and what we are to be about as a "people called forth." The motto of our church and from its inception has been none other than the words of Christ Jesus: "That they may all be one." That prayer of Christ may eventuate in the unity of all things—social, political, communal, global— but the initial point of Christ's prayer is that the unified body of disciples must represent the coming church.

We have tapped the resources of culture and society in the effort to address the crisis of disunity we face, only to find, at every point, that collective effort to have been a failed enterprise! This could eventually prove to be more than a time (chronologically speaking) of crisis for the church, it could also hold within it an opportunity (*kairos*) for a more decisive biblical and theological dialog to develop an ecclesiology that speaks more creatively and constructively to the ecumenical core of our character as church. I respectfully submit this book as an initial and tentative contribution toward that dialog and to that end. The creedal affirmation of the church as *one, holy, catholic, and apostolic* cannot be replaced by any other set of defining characteristics intended, even with the best of intentions, to communicate a contemporary identity of the church deemed more suitable to the tastes of seekers, without rupturing connections with the classic confessional heritage of the church and corrupting the comprehension of the church's *ecumenical* distinctiveness. This classic definition of the church was not hammered out on the anvil of "self-preservation" so much as forged in the fires of the need to provide a biblically attuned and theologically ideal image of the church as God in Christ, under the power of the Holy Spirit, created her to be and become.

It is, therefore, *this* vision-and-vocation of the church that should be the point of entry for any and every discussion concerning the disposition and direction of the United Church of Christ as church. I contend that in practicing a kind of *ressourcement* (a return to the original sources), the United Church of Christ can create an ecclesiological identity more faithful to her ecumenical heritage and certainly more vibrant than any uniqueness established on the principles of marketing, management, or in conformity to contemporary cultural, political, and/or social agendas. In the contemporary climate, the church has been marginalized, or in some cases has chosen to relegate herself to marginalization! We face a condition placing the church at risk of becoming dangerously inaccessible to the "worldliness" of the world. This is also a circumstance in which the ecumenical agenda could be taken up once again with renewed vigor and as a form of mission; a renewed energy for mission is being fostered, just as in 1910, and many are beginning to wonder how we too can "win the world for Christ." Cultural accommodation has not proven to be a successful methodology for the development of missionary outreach to a "world come of age," to employ the phrase coined by Pastor Dietrich Bonhoeffer.[5]

---

5. In a letter addressed to Eberhard Bethge, dated June 30, 1944, Bonhoeffer described circumstances eerily similar to our own contemporary setting; he wrote: "My starting point was that God is being increasingly pushed out of a world come of age,

Finally, I would call the reader's attention to the title of this book, "*An* Ecumenical Ecclesiology." It is intentional to the degree that I am offering one proposal and suffer no delusion that my suggestion is a panacea, bringing all conversation to an end. It is, as I have stated, a contribution to what I hope will be a more constructive and engaging exchange on the identity of the United Church of Christ as we seek to become ever more faithful to our call as an ecumenical community, enriching the formation of conciliar identity among members of local congregations, reclaiming the power of our God-given vision-and-vocation, and inspiring the wider church.

---

from the realm of our knowledge and life and, since Kant, has only occupied the ground beyond the world of experience. On the one hand, theology has resisted this development with apologetics and taken up arms—in vain—against Darwinism and so on; on the other hand, it has resigned itself to the way things have gone and allowed God to function only as deus ex machina in the so-called ultimate questions, that is, God becomes the answer to life's questions, a solution to life's needs and conflicts." Bonhoeffer, *Letters and Papers from Prison*, 450.

Having participated in one of the Oxford round table discussions where the theme was the nature and substance of the debate between science and theology, with particular focus on approaches to the theory of evolution, I can testify to the relevance of Bonhoeffer's insight. The church has every good reason to engage in open and constructive conversation with representatives of both the arts and sciences, yet at the same time has a fundamental obligation to Christ as Lord to pursue real advances in visible unity, in commitment to his command and in recognition of the fundamental unity of all things in Christ—things sacred, secular, and scientific (Eph 1:20–23).

1

The Issue

In an article entitled "The Church, Encounter with Christ," Romano Guardini offered this appraisal of the concept of "church" in Protestantism: "I scanned more than fifty years of theoretical study and personal exchange, and the fact of Protestantism's vital relationship to Sacred Scripture was once again emphatically clear to me. Yet, equally clear was the fact that Protestantism's relationship to 'Church' was very indefinite. As a matter of fact, as often as I have heard the word Church employed in a Protestant context, I have never been able to determine its precise connotation."[1] Hyperbole? Perhaps. But one cannot ignore the paucity of ecclesiological reference in *much* of Protestantism, with the possible exception of the twentieth century (often called the century of the church). It is not merely a question of defining the concept of church, but rather the lack of attention given to defining the nature of church in Protestantism to the *one, holy, catholic, and apostolic church*. The critical observation of Romano Guardini takes on immediate relevance when we turn to the United Church of Christ.

A critical issue facing the United Church of Christ (hereafter UCC) is directly related to a persistent theological challenge: an imprecise ecclesiology. The absence of a distinct ecclesiology is confirmed in a confusion of identity experienced by many who claim a commitment

---

1. Guardini, "The Church," 16.

to this conciliar community of faith.² The UCC is a conciliar fellowship³ with a dissimilar membership—a diversity of people from an equally colorful array of cultural, ethnic, social, and geographical backgrounds.⁴ However, this feature of diversity only sharpens the edge of my argument regarding the question of conciliar identity and necessitates greater specificity in the formation of a Christian self-understanding among members of the local congregation. Additionally, a mistaken belief vis-à-vis the relationship between *unity* and *diversity* together with what has been called an "ecclesiological deficit"⁵ sharpens the edge of the identity issue, adding further warrant to my contention.

2. In his study of the UCC as an "exercise in ecumenicity," theologian and church historian Louis H. Gunnemann offers the following observation: " 'Who we are?' is a question arising not only from confusion and uncertainty . . . but also especially in the United Church of Christ, from the absence of a common language of faith by which the community of faith is identified as church." In a footnote, Gunnemann offers this clarification: "A common language of faith can serve as a means of identity only when it is 'catholic' (universal) in its derivation and expression." Commenting on the issue of identity in the UCC, Gunnemann writes: "The question of identity is disconcerting on two levels . . . church identity has a social as well as religious importance. The need at this time, however, is not primarily social; it is essentially a matter of faith identity. Corporate confession of ecclesial identity requires a common language of faith . . . what is at stake is the credibility of the United Church of Christ." Gunnemann, *United and Uniting*, 4–5.

3. I prefer the term "conciliar fellowship" as an ecclesiological referent for the UCC under the conviction that it is a more fitting description of the church's core characteristic than is implied in the traditional designation of *denomination*. Moreover, the term "conciliar fellowship" reflects the UCC's association with the Church catholic: "The term 'conciliar fellowship' has been frequently misunderstood. It does not look towards a conception of unity different from that full organic unity sketched in the New Delhi document, but is rather a further elaboration of it. The term is intended to describe an aspect of the life of the one undivided Church *at all levels*. In the first place, it expresses the unity of the church separated by distance, culture, and time, a unity which is publicly manifested when the representatives of these local churches gather together for a common meeting. It also reflects a quality of life within each local church, it underlines the fact that true unity is not monolithic, does not override the special gifts given to each member and to each local church, but rather cherishes and protects them." Fifth Assembly of the WCC, "Report of Section II: What Unity Requires," Nairobi, 1975, 110–11.

4. Roger L. Shinn has defined this diversity in terms of "a few paradoxes characteristic of the United Church of Christ." He goes on to define these paradoxes in their specific dynamic as "language, spiritual ancestry, and geographical distribution." Shinn, *Unity and Diversity*, 1–2.

5. For an insightful analysis of the impact this "ecclesiological deficit" had on the first three decades of the UCC's ecumenical journey as a "united and uniting" church,

Both within the UCC and among the confessional bodies with which the UCC has entered into ecumenical agreement, the phrase "*united and uniting*"[6] has been a trademark feature of the church. An ecumenical agenda has been indispensable to the church's identity since its founding in 1957; even so, ecumenicity has not contributed to the formation of an attending ecclesiology and accompanying conciliar identity recognizable at any level, much less the level of the local congregation.[7] As a consequence, the promise of ecumenicity, as an essential resource in the advance of conciliar identity throughout the church, and beginning in the setting of the local congregation, has not yet been realized.[8] One of the objectives of this book is to explore and discuss viable approaches to rectify this situation.[9]

AVOIDING DENOMINATIONAL CATEGORIES

My purpose cannot be achieved using denominational markers and associated language. In principle, I elect to avoid the use of the term "denominational" in reference to the UCC because I consider such classification deficient in representing the richness of the traditions of our conciliar fellowship, as well as the ecumenical vision-and-vocation

---

see Gunnemann, *United and Uniting*, 27–40.

6. "The community of faith that was named the United Church of Christ in 1957 has exhibited from the beginning some significantly formative ecclesial ideas, expressed in the intention to be a *united* and a *uniting church*." Ibid., 3.

7. "The possibilities and problems experienced in the formation of the United Church of Christ ecclesial model clearly suggest significant unfinished business. The most urgent of these matters . . . is a full and intensive examination of ecclesiological principles, presupposed but never fully implemented, in the covenantal instrument devised for the shaping of our life as God's mission in the world—the Constitution and Bylaws." Ibid., 155.

8. "In fact, it is in the local church that the experience of being *united* and *uniting* has been remote and somewhat unreal. In the absence of opportunity and intentional effort, the experience has been denied in many local churches that continue to be identified solely by their original Congregational Christian or Evangelical and Reformed name. A persistent and subtle parochialism easily enshrines old habits and perspectives, extending their influence into succeeding generations." Ibid., 16.

9. "Ecumenical discussions of the substance of faith, as they relate to the United Church of Christ self-understanding as church, inevitably become a time of testing and learning. As a people on an ecclesial journey we are challenged at every turn, not to justify ourselves but to clarify and to be clear about the requirements of the ecumenical vocation we have claimed. To be a 'united and uniting church' requires special diligence lest too much or too little is claimed." Ibid., 40.

of the UCC. Moreover, in reference to the UCC, denominational language merely impedes ecumenical engagements and further complicates issues of conciliar identity formation among members of the local congregation.[10]

As stated above, the UCC came into existence in 1957; in that same year a prominent theologian, H. Richard Niebuhr, wrote the following on the historical expansion of denominationalism:

> The history of schism has been a history of Christianity's defeat. The church which began its career with the promise of peace and brotherhood for a distracted world has accepted the divisions of the society it hoped to transform and has championed the conflicts it had thought to transcend. In its denominational aspect, at least, it has become part and parcel of the world, one social institution alongside many others . . . more frequently conditioned by other cultural tendencies than conditioning them.[11]

It could be argued that Niebuhr's analysis is dated, his conclusions flawed, his observations irrelevant. Yet in response I would offer one of several remarks made by contributors to the *Princeton Proposal for Christian Unity*. The document is the product of a three-year study undertaken by a broad range of theologians and ecumenists. The stated purpose of this gathering was "to reflect on the present situation and future possibilities of modern ecumenism" and "to speak to all churches, out of shared concern for the founding ecumenical imperative 'that they all may be one . . . so that the world may believe' (John 17:21)."[12] In the third section of the published statement and in language resonant with that of Niebuhr quoted above, the drafters of the *Princeton Proposal* state that:

---

10. Louis Gunnemann has written: "In all honesty, it must be stated, that although it sought at the beginning to be a new form of church life, the UCC has become in most ways simply another 'denomination.' " We promote the formation of conciliar identity because "as the *quality of life* of the united church, [it] refers to the acceptance of a new identity, in which reconciliation, and a new experience of freedom, predominate. As a conciliar community the church is able to demonstrate freedom and wholeness in a society where alienation breeds hostility, and where over-zealous individualism is expressed in adversarial relationships. As a united church demonstrates and is recognized by this conciliar quality, it becomes a sign of hope for the unity of humankind." Ibid., 150, 158.

11. Niebuhr, *Social Sources of Denominationalism*, 264–65.

12. Braaten and Jenson, *In One Body*, 5–6.

our churchly identities lack the winnowing and transformative power of the gospel. Our missions in a particular place all too easily enter into complex collusions with divisions of class, culture, ethnicity, or status already present there. Rather than reconciling the divided, the gathering of men and women into churches may reinforce their divisions . . . and we run the danger of denominational loyalty by "boasting" of something more unique than the gospel of Jesus Christ.[13]

Among the suggestions made within this same document is guidance pertinent to my purpose:

No matter how we understand the roles, structures, or status of our churches, denominations, and fellowships of faith, we must incorporate the imperative of unity into our mission. We must yearn for the fullness of reconciliation and mutual love promised in the return of our Lord. And most importantly, we must seek to discern the forms of communion that might draw us together in joint mission.[14]

My interest is not simply to replace denominational identifications, nor chiefly to promote a "joint mission," though I acknowledge the merit of such goals. I seek to recover, for our own time and place (that is, the local church in the wider church), the ecumenical vision-and-vocation that characterizes the UCC as a conciliar fellowship. I believe that our church's ecumenical location is *the* defining attribute in the formation of a conciliar identity among members that is in congruence with a church defined by the expression "*united* and *uniting*." If the assertion of being a "*united* and *uniting*" church has no real meaning to the person seated in the pew on a Sunday morning, then its life and genuine effectiveness will be severely limited, if not ultimately pointless.

The founders of the UCC never intended the ecumenical agenda to be optional for members of the local congregation or the wider na-

13. Ibid., 34–35. Douglas John Hall writes: "North American denominationalism is simply a *scandalon*—and not even a false scandal, but a real one. It literally betrays the gospel and makes a mockery of Jesus' high priestly prayer 'that they may be one' (John 17)." Hall, *Confessing the Faith*, 101. I would also add the comment of Bernard Lambert quoting another: "The Church must . . . be delivered from the limitations of denominationalism which prevent it from showing itself in its catholicity. The true nature of the Church must again be freed from that which conceals it, just as, in the sixteenth-century, the Reformers affected a similar grand ecumenical awakening." Lambert, *Ecumenism*, 97.

14. Braaten and Jensen, *In One Body*, 36–37.

tional ministries. More than three decades ago, in a document adopted by the General Synod and in unequivocal terms, the call was issued to the whole church to acknowledge its ecumenical mandate:

> Ecumenicity is not an option for us; rather it is a mandate that prohibits a restrictive view that would separate mission from unity, or unity from mission. Whenever we view ecumenicity as mainly cooperative planning and action rather than as the name for those active steps toward the goal of church union for the union of all humankind, we trap ourselves in the false dichotomy of mission vs. unity or unity vs. mission. The goal is the *union* of the church and the *union* of creation, and mission and unity are the processes to be followed in reaching the goal. We affirm that these belong irrevocably together in God's order.[15]

The words "the goal of church union for the union of all humankind" together with those asserting that the "goal (of ecumenicity) is the *union* of the church and the *union* of creation" are essential to any proper understanding of the overall goal implicit in ecumenicity as a directive. This objective too is Christ centric, as in the assertion of Bradford Littlejohn regarding the incarnational nature of John W. Nevin's catholic theology: "Christ comes . . . as the full flowering of the life of the world and of the human nature." In the words of Nevin:

> Here then (with the incarnation), as before said, we reach the central FACT, at once primal, in the constitution of the world. All nature and all history flow towards it, as true and proper end, or spring from it as their principle and ground. The incarnation, by which divinity and humanity are joined together, and made one, in a real inward and abiding way, is found to be the scope of all God's counsels and dispensations in the world. The mystery of the universe is interpreted in the person of Jesus Christ.[16]

---

15. Gunnemann, *United and Uniting*, 189.

16. Littlejohn, *Mercersburg Theology*, 154. On the following page is a quote taken from the writings of the Roman Catholic theologian, Henri De Lubac, which captures in even more graphic terms the contention being made for the centrality of the wider goal of ecumenicity. De Lubac wrote: "The Creator and the Redeemer, the Church adds, as one and the same God; therefore there can be no conflict between their works, and it is to stray from the true path to believe the second can be magnified at the expense of the first. The Word that became incarnate to renew and complete all things is also he who 'enlighteneth every man that cometh into this world.' *Dominus naturalia legis non dissolvit, sed extendit et implevit.* Just as he did, his messengers come not to destroy but to accomplish; not to lay waste, but to raise up, transform, make holy." De Lubac, *Splendor of the Church*, 155.

CONCILIAR IDENTITY

The formation of conciliar identity with distinctive features and of vital consequence to the UCC is not to be misconstrued as another form of exclusivism or what would be worse, triumphalism. The proposed identity is not solely the prerogative of the UCC or any body of believers claiming to be a *united* and *uniting* church. As most churches desire to foster faithfulness and obedience to Christ, and Christ expressed an appeal for the unity of his church (John 17), the formation of a conciliar identity is an open challenge to every Christian community.

However, the promise of the UCC is located in its ecumenical agenda.[17] Conciliar identity contributes to the promotion of the ecumenical agenda on at least two fronts: (1) as counteractive to the divisive propensity among ecclesiological opinions to characterize the Christian community and accompanying identity in the restrictive terminology of a particular confessional or doctrinal position,[18] and (2) as paradigmatic of the proleptic fulfillment of Christ's prayer for "oneness" (John 17:20–23), a foreshadowing of the unity that is foremost a gift of God and to which the Church catholic is summoned to give visible expression.[19]

Michael Kinnamon argues that "faithfulness to the gospel means expressing in word and deed the given oneness of the church. To be indifferent to the unity of the church as the body of Christ is to be indifferent

---

17. "The historical context provided by the ecumenical movement *keeps our perspectives of understanding in a universal, holistic framework* that counters the new parochialism in American church life. Parochialism in church life has always been a persistent distortion, exhibited in exclusivistic congregationalism and denominationalism. Ecumenical vision and commitment provide the countervailing energies to that distortion." Gunnemann, *United and Uniting*, 6–7.

18. "There *are* times when Christians must take sides against sisters and brothers in the church. But even in such moments, our understanding of church must be shaped more by theology than by politics. Even in such moments we must recognize that the 'them' we oppose are, in some fundamental way, 'us.' The ecumenical church cannot fear controversy or confrontation, for that is paralyzing, but it must hate division because the story by which we live tells us that we have been linked in communion with persons we otherwise would shun. Nothing else can testify so powerfully that our trust is in God, not in the things or even the communities of our devising." Kinnamon, *Vision of the Ecumenical Movement*, 21–22.

19. "The ecumenical era marks radical changes in ecclesial self-understanding in which the accents fall on the divine intention for the church rather than upon definitions of the 'true' church . . . the formation of the United Church of Christ was an explicit attempt to give expression to that new orientation." Gunnemann, *United and Uniting*, 7.

to Christ.' "[20] We should not encourage unity at the expense of diversity, nor commend a diversity that hinders expressions of unity.[21] There is no one church that can allege to have grasped the whole of the gospel, and none that can profess to have exhaustively observed the depth of the gospel's demands. It is, however, characteristic of a conciliar fellowship to continue to learn from other Christian communities[22] seeking unity in the midst of diversity, for the sake of both church and world.

The identity being advocated is not idealistic, as though advancing conciliar identity could resolve all causes of division in the wider church. Realistically, any form of Christian identity will be rudimentary and bounded by the eschatological imperative (see Eph 4:4–13; 1 Cor 13:12).[23] Ecumenical formation is "an ongoing process of learning within the various local churches and world communions, aimed at informing and guiding people in the movement which—inspired by the Holy Spirit—seeks the visible unity of Christians."[24] The ecumenical agenda must not remain the sole province of professionals and ecumenical officers at the national and global levels; the formation of conciliar identity in the local congregation is vital to responsible involvement of lay people in furthering the ecumenical ministry and mission under the mandate of the Lord Jesus Christ.

In an article written in 1993, Konrad Raiser lamented the marginalization of the laity in contemporary ecumenical activities. This unfortunate lapse in lay participation "is all the more striking because

---

20. Kinnamon, *Vision of the Ecumenical Movement*, 108.

21. The Lutheran ecumenist Harding Meyer cautions against the tendency in contemporary ecumenical circles to place greater emphasis than necessary on the value of protecting diversity. He writes that "the idea of legitimate and necessary diversity seem . . . to have such a preponderance that the crucial question about the limits of diversity and with it the struggle for overcoming church-dividing differences—an absolutely central and necessary concern of the ecumenical movement—recedes into the background." Meyer, *That All May Be One*, 140.

22. In the "Decree on Ecumenism of the Second Vatican Council, 1964," the term "dialogue" is used to describe that process of mutual learning in which "each explains the teaching of his [her] communion in greater depth and brings out clearly its distinctive features. Through such dialogue everyone gains a truer knowledge and more just appreciation of the teaching and religious life of both Communions." Kinnamon, *Vision of the Ecumenical Movement*, 27.

23. "All Christians recognize a distinction between the *una sancta*, the eternal church that needs no renewal, and the historical church that stands everywhere and always in need of it." Ibid.

24. Gros, Meyer, and Rusch, *Growth in Agreement II*, 886.

'laity' was an ecumenical keyword only a generation ago. Since then the passionate enthusiasm of the early ecumenical movement—which in several important respects saw itself as a lay movement—has somewhat abated."[25] This notable absence of lay involvement in ecumenism is all the more pressing an issue for the UCC, which represents "a testing" of the ecumenical "vision."[26] That is not to imply that should the UCC fail, the ecumenical vision is likewise doomed to failure; the work of unity is far greater than any particular branch of the Christian family tree currently engaged in the mission.

Likewise, the survival of the UCC, as a denomination, is not at issue; whether we can remain faithful to the ecumenical vision-and-vocation of our beginnings without a more active involvement on the part of the laity is paramount. Agreements can be made, covenants signed, and mission projects shared, but if the ecumenical mission of the UCC does not absorb the laity, it will be of limited value. Greater merit will be discovered in educating the members of the local congregation to appreciate and adopt the ecumenical heritage that is their own. Education of this kind may also achieve a level of ecclesiological clarity:

> If the UCC is truly committed to the ecumenical mandate, critical examination of its own structure and claims is simply an expression of the conciliar process at the heart of that movement, [in] that ecumenical conciliar process the UCC may indeed be called to undergo a radical transformation in which the deleterious effects of its ecclesiological confusion can be removed from its commitment to the mission of unity.[27]

---

25. Raiser, "Laity in the Ecumenical Movement," 375.
26. Gunnemann, *United and Uniting*, 7.
27. Ibid., 150.

2

The Vital Importance of the Local Congregation

ADDRESSING THE INSTITUTIONAL STRUCTURES of the national church is not my first concern, which may cause some to question the intrinsic value of my case because the goal seems too narrowly focused. However, attending to the complexity of issues facing the national church's ecumenical agenda would be impractical and needs to be reserved for another day and another dialog. Nor do I believe for a moment that what I offer will have an immediate effect on current ecumenical efforts at the national level. But in order for the revitalization of our founding ecumenical vision-and-vocation to succeed, effort, energy, and education must be channeled through the life of the local congregation.[1]

Materials and recommendations to further ecumenical relationships at the local level have been offered by our national ministries. A collection of informational cards intended to strengthen all areas of leadership in the local church, and published under the auspices of the Office for Church Life and Leadership of the UCC, contains one card devoted to ecumenical efforts at the local level. "Ecumenism in Your Community" is helpful in what it offers, but in essence it offers far too little to be genuinely effective. The following counsel is offered regarding local ecumenical engagements:

> Local councils of churches enable Christians to work together toward a goal that one congregation or denomination would have

---

1. In his own assessment of the past accomplishments and future direction of the ecumenical movement, Michael Kinnamon writes: "Much has been accomplished over the past generation through official church-to-church dialogues and much has been gained over the past two generations through the official participation of churches in conciliar ecumenism. The task for the next generation will be to celebrate and deepen such church involvement *while also* making room for volunteer lay-led movements, and emphasizing education for ecumenism among the laity." Kinnamon, *Vision of the Ecumenical Movement*, 85.

difficulty accomplishing alone. Sometimes this means that not only are denominational barriers broken but so are racial and ethnic ones. In addition to banding together for service projects, such as support for peace efforts, housing projects, disaster relief and hunger programs, such councils support radio and television programs. Ecumenical cooperation broadens horizons, deepens convictions and increases opportunities for significant service. In the process, we seem to be moving closer to the unity which Christ prayed for.[2]

While helpful, these suggestions cannot adequately equip members of the local congregation for a more proactive role in local ecumenical ministries. My thirty years of pastoral experience confirm Michael Kinnamon to be correct when he argues that local churches "are often all too ready to leave ecumenism to 'the council'—as if conciliar membership means that they have hired persons to be ecumenical for them. When this happens, councils lose their ecumenical significance."[3] We must equip the laity of the local congregation so that they can contribute to local ecumenicity, doing so with knowledgeable judgment and theological integrity.[4]

Cardinal Edward Idris Cassidy assesses why ecumenism has not yet captured the attention of the laity to the same degree that it has the clergy and why there has been little urgency in the pursuit of ecumenical unity: "The lack of understanding the ecumenical imperative" as well as "the urgency of the unity of the Church for the sake of the unity of humankind, is mainly due to a lack of ecumenical education and formation."[5] As Cassidy suggests, local churches should provide educational programs that are practical as well as cognitive in equipping the laity for responsible engagement in ecumenical endeavors: "Christians must be helped to understand that to love Jesus necessarily means to love everything Jesus prayed, lived,

---

2. "Ecumenism in Your Community," *The Leadership Collection*, card A-15.

3. Kinnamon, *Vision of the Ecumenical Movement*, 91.

4. This is not to suggest a prioritization of purposes, so that the formation of conciliar identity comes somewhere down the scale when compared with participation in local ecumenical efforts. As clearly stated, I hold confessional commitments, identity formation, and the ability to participate responsibly and knowledgably in ecumenical efforts in conjunction. I do so in agreement with Brinkman when he argues that "real catholicity requires the communion of all local churches and pertains to the identity of each local church and constitutes an essential quality of their communion together." Brinkman, *Progress in Unity?* 19.

5. Cassidy, "Ecumenical Education and Formation," 55.

died and was raised for, namely... the unity of his disciples as an effective sign of the unity of all peoples ... ecumenical formation [includes] the actual involvement in dialogue experience, individually and in community ... and participation in the whole ecumenical foundation process is crucial."[6]

The local congregation must be the point of ecumenical convergence.[7] The essential link between the individual member, the church "in each place," and the Church catholic, is expressed in several New Testament epistles (e.g. 1 Cor 12:12; Eph 1:22–23; 4:12–13). The individual member cannot be treated in isolation from the wider community of faith. The ecumenical vision-and-vocation critiques the expressions of individualism, isolationism, and relativism currently infecting the local congregation.[8] Transforming the perceptions and self-understanding of local church members can be a catalyst for considerable change at the national level as well. Anthony Robinson has argued that the primary purpose of the church is to change, to

> bring about change in people's lives.... The kind of change the church seeks to bring about can be further described in several phases. We seek to "make disciples of Jesus." We are in the business of "Christian formation." We want to change people in such a way that the Christian story of grace and response becomes the lens, the perspective, through which they can see and understand life. And although mainline Protestant churches may be reluctant to use the word, what I am talking about is 'conversion,' turning around, being born anew, changed, made new... followers of the One "who makes all things new."[9]

---

6. Ibid., 56.

7. "One problem with bilateral and multilateral dialogue reports is reception. How are the results of dialogues to be communicated to regions and localities in such a way that any challenge to fresh thinking and any encouragements to positive action towards greater unity can be accepted, and not appear as attempted impositions from on high? It would seem that the only way forward is to regard international dialogue reports as checks, balances, and stimuli to regional unity efforts; for in the last resort Christian unity is a matter of "all in each place," and the suggestions of others must, to be productive, become our own." Sell, *Reformed, Evangelical, Catholic Theology*, 239.

8. Commenting on the theme of "freedom and unity" from the 1975 assembly of the WCC, Michael Kinnamon affirms that "countless Christians have testified that knowledge of God's gracious acceptance frees us from [a] cramped life of self-confirmation, frees us to live no longer for ourselves or by ourselves—but for Christ and in the community of his disciples." Kinnamon, *Vision of the Ecumenical Movement*, 117.

9. Robinson, *Transforming Congregational Culture*, 32.

The Vital Importance of the Local Congregation 13

While mainline churches tended to shy away from the idea or experience of "conversion" in the twentieth century, the local congregation in pursuit of an ecumenical vision, and as an expression of conciliar fellowship, would do well to appropriate a *conversionist* model. In a helpful book coauthored by three Roman Catholic ecumenists, the authors state the connotation of conversion among participants in the ecumenical movement:

> The process of conversion is the process of being drawn more deeply into the mystery of the triune God. The full conversion of the human person involves the outward and the inward person and the congruity between the two. It involves works of love and interior experiences of God's own presence. It involves the sacraments and worship, and disciplines of thought, study, and prayer. And it involves an increasing ability to see the many ways that God is at work reconciling the world to himself in the diversity of Christian communities. Conversion is essential to the ecumenical dimension of identity.[10]

There is also the corporate dimension of conversion, so that "not only personal failings in charity, wisdom, or moral conduct of individuals are to be approached honestly, but the household of the church, the ways of articulating the faith, and of carrying out its tasks may need to be renewed."[11] Konrad Raiser claims that the unity of the church will remain a distant goal without a genuine conversion—that is a turning away from the negative images and exclusive identities fostered by the anathemas and mutual condemnations of the past—and a common turning to God in Christ as the only true foundation of our unity as Christians and churches. We are called to receive this gift in the spirit of renewal and conversion of the heart and mind.[12]

In a similar manner, Darrell L. Guder argues for the centrality of conversion as an ongoing process in the life of the local congregation: "It is indeed a work of God's Spirit when we recognize that under the guidance of the Word of God the church must constantly experience re-shaping, re-forming. It might well be, however, that re-forming is not enough. In view of our reductionism and cultural captivity, it might be

---

10. Gros, McManus, and Riggs, *Introduction to Ecumenism*, 94.
11. Ibid., 106.
12. Raiser, *To Be the Church*, 60.

evidence of greater spiritual honesty if we were to describe ourselves as churches continually needing conversion."[13]

Throughout his book, Guder contends that the most suitable theological model for understanding the mission of the church is the incarnation.[14] Christians are formed by the convictional language of their faith, and in learning to speak and live that same language, each Christian finds ways to say what he or she believes and has the opportunity to do so. This happens through the "spiritual conversion" of the community, which may and should be constantly practiced. The members of the congregation need constantly to be helped to "say their faith" when they are together, so that they can learn how to say it when they are apart—that is, when they are "the sent-out people of God in mission."[15] Members in the local congregation of the UCC need first to learn and come to appreciate the sheer power implicit in the language of an ecumenical faith, as "conversionist" or "transformational," so that as "the sent-out people of God in mission" they can effectively participate in local ecumenical ministries that will make visible the unity we share in Christ as a foretaste of the *oikoumene*.[16]

All too often hostilities leading to further divisions in the wider church as well as the local congregation have little to do with the kinds of theological and confessional issues one discovers in ecumenical engagements. In large part, such divisions are due to an exaggerated focus on what Guder calls "single-issue battles such as abortion, human sexuality, capital punishment, and pluralism": "Yet, the real challenge for the church is not so much these difficult problems as it is the way we deal with them. Clarity about the church's missionary nature and honesty about its need for continuing conversion will enable us to deal with these problems in more authentically evangelizing ways."[17]

---

13. Guder, *Continuing Conversion of the Church*, 150.

14. Ibid., 191–92, 202–4. I note the similarity of this position to that of the Mercersburg theology, which stresses the transformational power evident in the incarnational nature of the language of faith, while distancing itself from the "anxious bench" notion of a conversionist model.

15. Ibid., 161.

16. "The Reformed protest is in the interests of the catholic gospel and of the church as already one in Christ. The visible manifestation of that unity is to be a sign of the ultimate goal: the realization of the unity of the *oikoumene* in Christ." Sell, *Reformed, Evangelical, Catholic Theology*, 129.

17. Ibid., 167. In a similar fashion, Douglas John Hall argues for the continuing con-

Our witness and mission as a conciliar fellowship is much wider than concern with these "single-issue battles" would suggest. In the desire to recover our ecumenical vision-and-vocation we must not disconnect witness from mission or mission from witness, as the two are inherently interdependent. What Darrell Guder has attributed to local congregations in general is applicable in particular to those of the UCC as a conciliar fellowship: "The promised Holy Spirit can empower every mission community to use its redeemed creativity to discover what the specific shape of its agenda will be. What connects all local congregations to one another and forms the church catholic is the dominical mandate: You shall be my witnesses."[18] As a conciliar fellowship, our fundamental witness is to the gospel of reconciliation and in particular to the further promotion of unity among churches, even in local communities, not merely as testimony to our commitment to the wider ecumenical endeavor (though it reflects such commitment), but even more so in obedience to the prayerful word and petition of Christ (John 17:22–24).

The corporate nature of confession and the need for a "continuing conversion" are directly related to the recovery of our ecumenical vision and in accord with our Reformed heritage. Alan Sell makes reference to the Mercersburg church historian, Philip Schaff, who once issued a prophetic word to the church: "The problem of Christian union . . . is one of the great problems of the nineteenth century, and will work itself out in various ways until the great prophecy of the one Shepherd and one flock be fully realized." Sell adds: "That day is not yet, but in working for it the Reformed are in no sense stepping outside of their tradition." Moreover, he asserts that it is "consistent with [the] understanding of the

---

version of the church and the necessity for conversion to be communal and not merely individuated: "To its credit, evangelical Christianity in North America has retained this awareness and assumes 'conversion,' involving overpowering consciousness of personal sin, as the normal mode of entry into the community of faith. Unfortunately, its retention of the individual dimensions of this experience is seldom accompanied by any profoundly social dimension ('I dwell in the midst of a people of unclean lips,' Isa. 6:5), but at least the recognition that new hope entails a radical break with false hope and untruth is still present in this tradition. In the remnants of mainline churches, even personal metanoia is rare, and it is often caricatured or ridiculed. One can enjoy full membership in such communities of faith without ever having to confront the inauthenticity of one's own life, let alone the 'unclean lips' of the 'people' to which one belongs." Hall, *Confessing the Faith*, 467.

18. Guder, *Continuing Conversion of the Church*, 180.

catholicity of the church that the Reformed should strive for the fuller manifestation of Christian unity."[19]

BELIEFS AND PRACTICES[20]

My recommendation is that we promote practices congruent with those ecumenical factors said to be characteristic of a conciliar fellowship and the attending conciliar identity. Theologians Craig Dykstra and Dorothy Bass speak of a basic relationship between beliefs and practices, contending that Christian faith is intrinsically a "way of life" rather than mere intellectual assent to a body of abstract theological concepts. This "way of life" must be learned over time through processes that entail drinking long and often from the deep wells of the catholic tradition of the church.[21]

Christian practices imply "particular understandings, beliefs, events, behaviors, actions, relationships, inquiries, and skills"; however, they are not meant to summarize the whole of Christian life. The promotion of conciliar identity and the specific practices associated with that identity configuration does not imply that this identity constitutes the whole of any one person's self-understanding. My contention is that this "distinctive understanding of Christian practices focuses on practices as the constituent elements in a way of life that becomes incarnate" when members of the local congregation "live in the light of and in response to" particular characteristics of ecumenicity.[22]

Elaborating the essentials of Christian practices, Dykstra and Bass affirm that (a) "Christian practices . . . involve a profound awareness, a deep knowing" and (b) they are "social and historical" practices that "people engage in together over time."[23] The former implies that beliefs

---

19. Sell, *Reformed, Evangelical, Catholic Theology*, 112, 113.

20. It is of vital importance to reiterate the essential connection between the content of what is believed or confessed and the work of discipleship in a ministry of reconciliation in pursuit of visible signs of unity among churches in the local setting. As Sell has said, it is for each local church to recognize that it "is called to live by and witness to the gospel of the atoning grace of the triune God, who ever addresses and reforms his people by the Spirit through the Word discerned in fellowship. If . . . churches are faithful to this evangel they will not fail to be catholic and apostolic; they will minister compassionately and joyously to the religious, material, and intellectual needs of their several constituencies, and to the needs of the greater family beyond their borders." Ibid., 244–45.

21. Dykstra and Bass, "Theological Understanding of Practices," 18.

22. Ibid., 18–29.

23. Ibid., 24, 26.

are to be internalized, influencing a practitioner's life beyond mere intellectual assent. The latter affirms that true Christian education should connect practitioners with the historical church (past), encourage participation in the corporate body as the context of faith development (present), and enable formation and enrichment of Christian identity over time (future).

Ecumenical connectedness with the *one, holy, catholic, and apostolic church* is reinforced as the practices of members of the local congregation are "intricately linked to" the Church catholic "as well as to the practices of communities long ago."[24] There's a vital connection between the beliefs one holds (as well as the form in which they are held), the Christian practices in which one participates as informed by those same beliefs, and the formation of conciliar identity. As theologian Ellen Charry has written, "Christian doctrine can guide the Christian life because it forms identity and character."[25]

I make no claim to novelty of thought; historically the UCC has sought to promote a critical relationship between faith, identity, and the ethical decisions one regularly faces. In his study of the theological meaning implicit in the *UCC Statement of Faith*, Roger Shinn claims that "any confession of faith that speaks to our time must look to the expression of faith in the practical decisions of personal and social life."[26] Christian life is never simply a matter of personal volition, nor is it purely emotional, nor merely cognitive. Christian life is an act of the whole person, as a member of the Church catholic, apparent in a set of practices and giving clear evidence of a developing sense of identity shaped and informed within the context of the *one, holy, catholic, and apostolic church*.[27]

---

24. Ibid., 27.

25. Charry, *By the Renewing of Your Minds*, 240.

26. Shinn, *Confessing Our Faith*, 20.

27. "The life of the community is the primary form of its witness, and it is also the equipper and supporter of each individual Christian in the practice of his or her vocation as witness for Christ. The community is, as ecclesia, called out and set apart for public witness, for demonstration before the world of the presence and power of Jesus the king. We must grapple with the problems presented by the institutional church, but there can be no biblically based theology of mission and witness which does not emphasize the centrality of the 'called out people' for that mission." Guder, *Continuing Conversion of the Church*, 68.

3

Ecumenicity and Conciliar Identity Formation

THE TERM ECUMENICITY IS of central importance to the whole of my proposal as it is to the formation of conciliar identity. In their volume referred to earlier, Gros, McManus, and Riggs sketch features implied in the term *ecumenicity* by reference to "four Gospel values." These four values imply what must now be done in light of the "history of division and reconciliation" endemic to the life of the wider church in general and to the ecumenical movement in particular.

In our own context and as a conciliar fellowship, the UCC is called to demonstrate those "four Gospel values" by (1) "humble repentance, including taking responsibility for the failings of our Christian ancestors and recognizing the failures on both sides of the division"; (2) acknowledging "human mistakes and failings" that need to be rectified "in our own time," while demonstrating a genuine "respect for the gifts of the Holy Spirit to the churches, even in their years of separation." We must (3) embrace the "biblical, theological, and liturgical renewal in the Church that can help heal the wounds of the past." Above all, (4) "God's call for unity should be at the center of our review of the Christian past."[1]

A concise description of ecumenicity is impeded by the fact that the ecumenical movement continues to be history in the making. Bilateral and multilateral dialogues, as processes for achieving concord, require openness. Shifts in direction and modifications have occurred in the effort to bring about agreements and shared ministries. Dialogues and ecumenical partnerships between the UCC and other confessional bodies remain tentative, creating a degree of diffidence to such agreements and pronouncements. These realities make an unqualified definition of ecumenicity problematic.

1. Gros, McManus, and Riggs, *Introduction to Ecumenism*, 9.

All the same, distinctive features have guided the selection of characteristics essential to conciliar identity formation. One such feature is implied in the characterization of the UCC as a *united* and *uniting* church. This ecclesiological standard insinuates facets of ecumenicity basic to one's identity as a member in the UCC:

> Living toward unity . . . is a way of characterizing the style of life of a united church. That . . . requires an intentionality that goes far beyond the adjustments in organizational habits so as to "get on" with the mission of the church. It (involves) fundamental rethinking of the requirements of the mission of the church in matters of faith and order, a process that could not be done in advance of union but is an ongoing task. It is indeed an ecclesial journey in which the UCC has had to give a fresh account of its faith in every new circumstance. Learning to be accountable to Christ and Christ's Body requires a radical transformation [read: "conversion"] for which many may not be ready. Nevertheless, that is what is necessary in living toward unity. Although there have been many faltering steps on the journey, the rightness of the way has been continually validated both in experience and in the wider Christian community.[2]

Many members in settings of the local congregation would be unfamiliar with these features of the UCC, which identify its character as a united and uniting church. We must now educate in ecumenicity, teaching members of the local congregation exactly what it means to be a member of a united and uniting church; equipping members (a good Pauline phrase!) for participation in the ecumenical vision-and-vocation of the UCC as a visible manifestation of "living toward unity." To be a member in a local congregation of the UCC is to be nurtured in a community of faith where "the quality of life" of the *united* church is evident in

> the acceptance of a new identity in which reconciliation and a new experience of freedom predominate. As a conciliar community the church is able to demonstrate freedom and wholeness in a society where alienation breeds hostility, and where over-zealous individualism is expressed in adversarial relationships. As a united church demonstrates and is recognized by this conciliar quality, it becomes a sign of hope for the unity of humankind. The United Church of Christ in its ecclesial journey has a special reason to explore more fully the meaning of conciliarity. Its heritage in conciliar Congregationalism and in the representative

---

2. Gunnemann, *United and Uniting*, 135.

form of government in the Evangelical and Reformed tradition yields important insights for being a *united* and *uniting* church.³

Some of the more commonly held attributes of ecumenicity, terms used to define the particulars of the ecumenical movement—for example, *koinonia, oikoumene,* and *missio Dei*—are also trademarks of a conciliar fellowship.⁴ Select features of ecumenicity can also serve as a lens through which to explore a variety of historical and theological attributes of the UCC, aiding in the formation of conciliar identity. Paul Fries advocates one way that churches of the Reformed heritage can enter into agreement or concord with other confessional bodies without losing their historical and theological integrity. He sets parameters for ecumenical engagements by the use of two other marks of ecumenicity:

> What do Reformed churches look for in other churches before agreeing to make a *covenant* of mutual recognition? Surely this: (1) that in the *varied forms* of faith and practice which prevail in other communions *Christ is communicated as content, norm, and object* of the church . . . and (2) a pneumatological ecclesiology [that] is confirmed by *plurality* and *mutability*.⁵

Conciliar identity formation advances along the lines of those confessional and theological "witnesses" of the Reformed tradition and Church catholic in which the centrality of Christ as "content, norm, and

---

3. Ibid., 58.

4. I contend that both the reclamation of our church's ecumenical vision-and-vocation and the concomitant conciliar identity will reinforce the perception of the church as a form of counterculture, witnessing to a prophetic reality at odds with the cultural tendency toward separatism, exclusivism, individualism, and isolationism. The ecumenical terminology of *koinonia, oikoumene,* and *missio Dei,* to name but three, identify the community of faith in terms foreign to the context of North American culture, but of universal familiarity in the Church catholic. This is not to suggest, however, that the local church disengage from the immediate culture; to deny any responsibility for the world and its deepest need for reconciliation would be to forfeit the very vision-and-vocation we are seeking to reassert. Guder states that Lesslie Newbigin "speaks of the need for the Christian communities to be culturally bilingual. As followers of Christ, they are being formed into distinctive communities speaking the language of faith rooted and informed by Scripture. Therefore, they share with all Christian communities the cross-cultural commonality that is the presence and rule of Jesus Christ. As they follow Christ, their language makes them, in many ways, distinctive within their communities. They are, as they learn Christ, more and more 'strangers and aliens' (1 Peter), 'resident aliens' and 'colonies' (Hauerwas and Willimon), 'contrast societies'(Lohfink)." Guder, *Continuing Conversion,* 94. George Lindbeck argues for "an ecumenical Christianity which is a creative community." See the intriguing hypothesis of Lindbeck in his *Church in a Postliberal Age,* 91–105.

5. Fries, *Unity of the Churches,* 160.

object" is clearly evident.[6] At the same time, one must consider those issues relevant to ecumenicity in general and to the UCC in particular, for example, "plurality and mutability."

THE CHURCH AS A CONCILIAR FELLOWSHIP: PERSONAL AND CORPORATE IN NATURE[7]

One of the lessons learned from recent ecumenical exchanges and the attention given to the nature of the church in historical perspective is the idea that the church exists to express the Christian life in both personal and corporate terms:

> The church is . . . a servant people of God's coming kingdom, "the sign held up before the nations." As a first-fruit of the kingdom the church takes sides with the weak, the poor and the alienated. This for the sake of involving all its members in a personal appeal to seek first of all the kingdom of God by being itself, as a collective whole, an instrument for the liberation of people in distress. An ecumenically conceived ecclesiology, therefore, must not be self-centered, triumphalistic or complacent, but should direct the churches' service to the world, to justice, peace and integrity of creation.[8]

Claiming that the church was created to be "Christ-in-community," Robert S. Paul states that the church is to be "a reconciled community expressing a ministry of reconciliation" and therefore "we cannot separate

---

6. "The gospel is the event of the incarnation, death, resurrection, and ascension of Christ. In this event God's work of salvation is carried out, and those who encounter this risen Christ are called and empowered to be his witnesses. Witness is therefore Christocentric." Guder, *Continuing Conversion*, 64.

7. The observations that follow in this section are based on an understanding of the intrinsic nature of the organic relationship between the personal and corporate dimensions in the conciliar fellowship, in which a conciliar identity is first formed and then nurtured: "Every Christian community should see itself as a community of missionaries. Its responsibility to them is to guide them to identify God's calling, to recognize the gifts and opportunities they have, to provide them the biblical and theological training to incarnate the gospel in their particular fields, and then to commission them to that ministry. Our structures of membership need to be transformed into disciplines of sending." Guder argues that "Christian existence is related to God's mission, into which Christians are called individually and corporately. For this to take place, a complete transformation of the lives of Christians is called for . . . the Christian community is to become 'a contrast society' (Lohfink)." Ibid., 178, 130. The fact that my own definition of mission focuses on the centrality of furthering the visible unity of the church in the local setting, and not the more broadly defined *missio Dei*, in no way diminishes the applicability of Guder's observation.

8. Brinkman, *Progress in Unity?* 28.

what we believe from how we act."[9] Because that is so, conciliar identity must include: (1) those ecumenical characteristics of the UCC integral to the formation of conciliar identity; and (2) connections between the content of an ecumenical feature and some paradigmatic issue clearly relevant to furthering *koinonia*[10] at the local level. In this way, we further understanding and enactment of the church as a conciliar fellowship. Martien Brinkman lists five characteristics of a conciliar fellowship, the following four of which bear decisively on the use we make of the term:

- Conciliarity may point to an essential *feature* of the church's nature and an important *pattern* of its common life.
- It may imply both the *fellowship* of the divided churches (*conseil*) and the *representative gathering* of the one church (*concile*).
- It may point both to the ultimate *goal* of unity and to the *means* towards this goal.
- It may refer to the *form* as well as to the *vision* of church unity.[11]

Conciliar identity is grounded in the concept of the *united* church as a conciliar fellowship, and Gunnemann recommends this ecumenical conceptualization as an appropriate model for the UCC: "The new model of church life for the UCC, confirmed in its own experience and in ecumenical relationships, is the emphasis on the *church as a conciliar fellowship*. Although never explicitly expressed in the UCC Constitution, the conciliar principle undergirds the covenantal assumption throughout."[12]

Michael Kinnamon does not employ the term *conciliar identity*. Nevertheless, his christological assertion of the church as a community of reconciliation, in obedience to the one Lord who frees and unites,

---

9. Paul, *Freedom with Order*, 127.

10. I use this biblical term, also used in and throughout ecumenical settings, in the way it has been presented by Martien Brinkman: "The recognition and acknowledgement of the complete church in the various local churches has especially been stimulated by the New Testament concept of koinonia. On the basis of this concept it becomes clear that every church that baptizes in the name of the Father, the Son and the Holy Spirit and conforms to the apostolic proclamation as handed down to us in Holy Scripture, already participates in this communion. Indeed, one can see here an instance of a real, albeit incomplete, union of the Christian churches, which also manifests itself already in each separate church." Brinkman, *Progress in Unity?* 23.

11. Ibid., 26–27.

12. Gunnemann, *United and Uniting*, 139.

resonates with the centrality of Christ and the ministry of reconciliation evident in the ecumenical ecclesiology I propose for the UCC: "Whenever Christians say 'Jesus Christ does this or that,' it is, in effect, a statement of our own agenda as the church. If Jesus Christ frees and unites, then we who confess to be his body must be free-ers and unite-ers ['ambassadors of reconciliation'] *and* must live in a way that demonstrates both freedom and unity. We desperately need a reformation, a renewal movement that calls us back to this essential truth."[13] The "reformation" or "renewal movement" Kinnamon invites, in particular as I envision it in the UCC, must begin at the grassroots level, requiring an educated membership in the local congregation, adequately equipped with ecumenical resources mined from their shared history and beyond the boundaries of the UCC.

There are few issues more prevalent in the pastoral conversations I have with young parents than their expressed concern for the way in which the children are becoming increasingly isolated as they spend more time with contemporary forms of communication, e.g., cell phones, iPods, computer, etc., and less time seeking to nurture relationships with friends on a more personal and immediate basis. At first blush, one may question the relevancy of this expressed concern to the discussion at hand, but it merely highlights the fact that we are all and each of us living in an era of increasing polarization, isolation, and eccentricity. I would argue that this same phenomenon, as the practical or technological manifestation of a postmodern mindset, has impacted the church in ways that have not yet come to full fruit and yet is clearly evident in the way members in general view their relationship to the church as an expression of their individual choice and volition, rather than as a direct consequence of their having been baptized or confirmed. As a result, members have difficulty appreciating what it means to "belong" and to be accountable to any one community, not to mention membership in the Church catholic!

We are living in a global village that has had, with few exceptions, a greater influence on the formation of individual identity than has the church; this same culture is shaped more by a postmodern mindset, where all truth claims are relative and all religious beliefs of equal merit, than by the richness of Christian tradition. In this environment, it becomes all the more imperative that *church* reaffirm her commitment to the richness of the faith "handed-on" through the *Church catholic* as the foundation of identity formation among church members.

13. Kinnamon, *Vision of the Ecumenical Movement*, 116–17.

4

Autonomy in the Polity of the UCC

THERE IS A NEED for renewal in commitment to the ecumenical vision-and-vocation of the UCC,[1] but in order to bring about both effective and sustained involvement of lay people in the ecumenical initiative of the UCC, deliberate attention must also be given to the importance of *autonomy*[2] in the polity of this conciliar fellowship.[3] Before pursuing this

---

1. I am in concurrence here with the insight of Douglas John Hall whose comment reiterates the conviction of the vision-and-vocation of the guiding lights of the UCC: "The fragmentation of the church is not only an institutional scandal, it is a theological scandal—a scandal of faith. This faith, after all, is centered in belief that, through the judging love and loving judgment of God in Christ, reconciliation, mutuality, community, 'oneness' has been made possible. The 'dividing wall of hostility' (Eph. 2:14) has been broken down; we are able to respond in love to love given. Unity here does not imply uniformity, but it does imply mutuality; and this gospel is rendered incredible, quite literally, unbelievable, in a situation in which Christians not only give no evidence at all of such mutuality but adamantly exclude one another, some openly, some more subtly." Hall, Confessing the Faith, 100–101.

2. "The principle of 'local church autonomy' had been conceived by the Puritans as a way of protecting local churches from ecclesiastical authority interfering with their response to the Word of God. However, as the nineteenth century progressed, 'autonomy' was no longer used simply in discussions of church polity. Autonomy had become one of the cornerstones of democracy. Some Congregationalists, who had come to identify themselves by the principle of absolute autonomy, failed to notice that autonomy was no longer used in its original way—to safeguard the freedom of a local church to respond to God's Word. Autonomy had become an absolute value, disconnected from its theological rationale. In fact, autonomy concerns ended up haunting the efforts of Congregational churches to realize their ecumenical vision for many years. In the 1940s and 1950s, when certain members and congregations within Congregational Christian Churches decided that they could not come together with members of congregations in the Evangelical and Reformed Church to create the United Church of Christ, they resisted for the same reason: they feared that church union would destroy the absolute autonomy of the local congregation." Zikmund, Living Theological Heritage, 6:13.

3. "The basic unit of the life and organization of the United Church of Christ is the

critical issue further, it needs to be stated at the outset that autonomy (that is, *auto-nomos* or "self-law") as a category of ecclesiological interest to the UCC cannot be divorced from the biblical declaration of the freedom afforded in Christ; while they are not one and the same, I would argue that any proper understanding of the roll of autonomy in the life of the church must be based on a full comprehension of and appreciation for the concept of "freedom in Christ" as found in the writings of Saint Paul (2 Cor 3:17; Gal 5:3). Even taken in the most literal sense of the term (that is, self-law), one must not assume the Christian "self" to be independent of Christ, but rather accountable to Christ as Lord, and should (at least in *this* instance) regard the term "law" as referring to the "law of Christ" (Gal 6:2), the law of love as defined by and fulfilled in Christ's person, word, and work.[4]

An imprecise definition of the autonomous nature of the local church in the covenantal polity of the UCC can be an obstacle to ecumenical efforts; correctly understood as a relationship bounded by covenantal responsibilities and commitments, autonomy is less likely to be an impediment.[5] A correct concept of the covenantal nature of the church is therefore vital to the successful encouragement and equipping of laity for ecumenical engagement at the local level. Roger Shinn has written:

Local Church." Constitution of the United Church of Christ, article 5, paragraph 9, 3.

4. In Gal 6:2, Paul writes, "Bear one another's burdens, and in this way you fulfill the law of Christ." The "law of Christ" as the law of love does not abrogate the commandments of God (in particular, the Decalogue), but is in fact the fulfillment of that same law, the whole of the law. In his response to the question of which commandment in the law is greatest, Jesus replied, "You shall love the Lord your God with all your heart, and with all your soul, and with all your mind. . . . And the second is like it: You shall love your neighbor as yourself. On these two commandments hang all the law and the prophets" (Matt 22:37, 39, 40). Jesus Christ embodies the fulfillment of both in perfection. Notice should be given as well to the place of "love" in both as necessary to fulfillment. Christians cannot divorce themselves from continued obedience to both the commandments of God and the triplex usus legis (i.e., the "threefold use of the law"); nevertheless, under the lordship of Christ, this obedience can also and often look like the necessity to bear one another's burdens. It may well be that members of the UCC come closest to the fulfillment of the "law of Christ" when they willingly, and in patient good will, bear the burdens of their ecumenical brothers and sisters as they seek faithful engagement with their own God-given and Spirit sustained vision-and-vocation.

5. "Within the United Church of Christ, the various expressions of the church relate to each other in a covenantal manner. Each expression of the church has responsibilities and rights in relation to the others, to the end that the whole church will seek God's will and be faithful to God's mission." Constitution of the United Church of Christ, article 3, paragraph 6, 2.

> The church is a covenant people. The meaning of the covenant has special importance in the United Church of Christ, because many of its local churches were established by Christians coming together and entering into covenant, declaring their purposes and accepting their responsibilities. Behind this practice lies the older meaning of "covenant" which is shared throughout the ecumenical church. The Christian covenant is not simply an agreement between consenting people, who are free to break it by mutual agreement. It is a covenant between people of faith and God, the Creator and Renewer of the church.[6]

There are evident challenges to be faced when embracing an ecumenical agenda.[7] Shinn maintains that loyalty to our ecumenical vision-and-vocation will mean "we are going to have to make some hard decisions about our identity" (recall the words of Bonhoeffer!) and reconsider "the relation of our belief in the freedom of the local church to our loyalty to Christ and the church universal."[8] In a similar fashion, the admonition of the *Princeton Proposal* recommends a realistic assessment of what is required in the renewal of ecumenical efforts among all Christians:

> No matter what our location in the scandal of Christian division is, no matter how we understand our responsibility for division, the burdens of disunity are shared by all. Therefore, no matter how we understand the roles, structures, or status of our churches, denominations, and fellowships of faith, we must incorporate the imperative of unity into our mission. We must rejoice in the gift of unity that God gives. We must yearn for the fullness of reconciliation and mutual love promised in the return of our Lord. And most importantly, we must seek to discern the forms of communion that might draw us together in joint mission.[9]

---

6. Shinn, Confessing Our Faith, 82–83.

7. Thomas E. Dipko writes: "On the difficult path to reform that the quest for Christian unity requires, the past can illumine our way without inhibiting the work of the Holy Spirit. One of the saints of the Reformed Church urged that 'the traditions of a church should be her inspiration, and not her limitation, in the effort to achieve God's purposes.' Our forebears in the nineteenth and twentieth centuries knew and loved their traditions, and again and again offered them to the larger service of the universal church. They acted on their willingness to see denominations die in order to open a way for the universal church to become more visibly manifest in history. Their legacy to a future that they could not clearly see is an unshakeable trust in God's care for the church across all time, the church always reforming, the church catholic against which the gates of hell will not prevail." Dipko, postscript for *Growing Toward Unity*, 760–61.

8. Shinn, Unity and Diversity, 26–27.

9. Braaten and Jenson, In One Body, 36–37.

Directing the attention of the local congregation to the ecumenical imperative of the UCC can stimulate a renewed sense of appreciation among members for what it means to remain committed to the ministry of reconciliation. Conciliar identity may possibly soften quarrels and reconcile factions among members of the wider UCC as well. A renewal of our ecumenical vision-and-vocation may also be a catalyst for a rediscovery of the deeper meaning of the Reformed principle of *ecclesia reformata et semper reformanda*.[10]

CHRIST AT CENTER

Conciliar identity is grounded in an ecumenical ecclesiology understood solely in terms of the center towards whom it moves and from whom it derives its existence. It is Christ at the center of the gathered community who ultimately defines, clarifies, empowers, and transforms identity, both individual and communal.[11] This is an affirmation of the UCC as stated in the preamble to the constitution: "The United Church of Christ acknowledges as its *sole* Head, Jesus Christ, Son of God and Savior."[12]

Christ *alone* is the original point of all mission, ministry, worship, devotional practice, sacramental participation, and genuine leadership, binding together the various Christian traditions, transcending all confessional differences.[13] Referring to the Heidelberg Catechism as "a doc-

---

10. In their introduction to a collection of essays on the identity and ecumenicity of the Reformed tradition, Wallace M. Alston Jr. and Michael Welker make the following pertinent comment: "It is characteristic of Reformed theology to be in constant search of the Reformed identity and to define this identity time and again. If the 'ecclesia reformata et semper reformanda' is to be true to its source and its calling, it must live in constant search for truth, it must be ready to repent and to learn, and it must be prepared to bear witness and to give account, time and time again, for its theological convictions and certainties." Alston and Welker, Reformed Theology, x. See also Guder, Continuing Conversion of the Church, 150–65.

11. Douglas John Hall defines the church as "that community of discipleship which is being brought to live the representative life of Jesus Christ in the world. The church is not a substitute community but a representative community. It does not take the place of the world, it exists on behalf of the world. It is not an elite but an elect community: that is, it is chosen for service and as a means, not an end." Hall, Professing the Faith, 524.

12. Constitution of the United Church of Christ, 2. (Emphasis mine.)

13. "The Church is catholic in its being, in its being in Christ. Where Jesus Christ is, there, too, is the Church catholic, in which, in all ages, the Holy Spirit makes people participants of Christ's life and salvation, without respect of sex, race and position. In each local church the fullness of grace and truth are present. Hence, real catholicity

ument of union in order to reconcile the divided confessional groups in the church," Eberhard Busch directs our interest to question and answer 54 of the catechism, which affirms that "the church does not gather, protect, and sustain itself, but rather Christ does all this."[14] The Heidelberg Catechism is generally valued as a resource for the creation of confirmation materials for use within many congregations of the UCC.

To affirm that Christ is at the center in any comprehension and delineation of the Church catholic is more than dabbling in theological terminology; such an affirmation is essential to an ecumenical ecclesiology and the formation of conciliar identity because this "center" is the ontological reality of the *church as church*, a confirmation of the conviction that this one alone keeps the church bound to a fulfillment of the petition for unity as found in Christ's prayer in the seventeenth chapter of John's Gospel. In other words, Christology is at the heart of an ecumenical ecclesiology because Christ is more than the head of the Church catholic, he is also and within the realities of its earthly existence, the sum and substance of the church's being as such. The Church catholic is an expansion of the incarnation as the presence of Christ in and for the world. There can be no ecumenical ecclesiology that ignores this essential theological and confessional conviction.

This is the fundamental reason why we should not embrace a comma as an identifying symbol for the UCC as church; it merely contradicts the central place of Christ in the church and risks becoming nothing less than an idolatrous affront to the Lord who commands both total devotion and focused worship. Should the cross of Christ no longer hold the central place as the prevailing symbol of our confessional community, we would be at risk of undermining the importance placed on the very foundation upon which the church itself has historically been grounded for more than two millennia (1 Cor 3:11).

The cross of Christ is not a dispensable symbol that we are free to take or leave at our leisure and with almost flippant disregard for the sacrifice and salvation it embodies for all Christians. The cross is not merely a historical event in the life of our Lord but is essential to his identity as Messiah and is therefore a trademark of the Church catholic

---

requires the communion of all local churches and pertains to the identity of each local church and constitutes an essential quality of this communion together." Brinkman, Progress in Unity? 19.

14. Busch, "Reformed Strength," 22, 25.

as well. I believe it borders on apostasy to select from any number of cultural symbols available to us one (for example, a comma) that is deemed to better represent the central characteristic of our conciliar fellowship than does the cross of Christ. To assume that such selection will have little or no effect on the furtherance of visible unity among other confessional bodies with whom we may be in dialog or seek to be in dialog is, it seems to me, the height of naivety.

One cannot emphasize enough the fact that the risen Christ makes use of his cross-wounds as marks of identification with his distraught—and yes—disbelieving disciples! The humanity assumed with the incarnation is not simply shed with suffering at Calvary; it is a glorified humanity in resurrection, ascension, and placement at the *right hand of God*. That same glorified humanity is shared in and with the members of the Church catholic, so that all who are baptized into the death of Christ and raised to new life (as new creation!) now share in the spiritual realities of that same glorified humanity. The whole of the Christian life as a member of Christ's body in the Church catholic is embraced by the whole of Christ's glorified humanity, so that the Church catholic realizes in her members the expansion of the incarnation in and for the world.

John Williamson Nevin in his classic book, *The Mystical Presence*, writes:

> The process by which Christ is formed in his people is not thus two-fold but single. It lays hold of its subject in each case, not in the periphery of his (or her) person, but in its inmost centre, where the whole (person), soul and body, is still one undivided life.... Christ's life as a whole is borne over into the person of the believer as a like whole.... The power of Christ's life ... works as a human life; and as such becomes a law of regeneration in the body as truly as in the soul.[15]

In his correspondence with the Corinthian church, the apostle Paul wrote, "For in the one Spirit we were all baptized into one body—Jews or Greeks, slaves or free—and we were all made to drink of one Spirit" (1 Cor 12:13). Also, in his letter to the Galatians, Paul declared, "As many

---

15. Littlejohn, Mercersburg Theology, 105. Even though his stated purpose is different from that of the current study, Littlejohn's book is of immense value to all who wish to explore the connections between Mercersburg theology and broader ecumenical concerns; particularly helpful is his discussion of the intriguing relationship between the writings of Nevin and Schaff and both the Anglo-Catholic and Eastern Orthodox traditions.

of you as were baptized into Christ have clothed yourselves with Christ. There is no longer Jew or Greek, there is no longer slave or free, there is no longer male and female; for all of you are one in Christ Jesus" (Gal 3:27–28). Both passages point to the transcendence, *in Christ*, of all former defining characteristics of personal and corporate identity, whether sociocultural or ethnic in origin or nature.

Even more startling is the apostle's assertion that gender, as a specific defining characteristic, has also been transcended (but not obliterated!). One could argue that because such defining characteristics have been transcended *in Christ*, the essential characteristic for both the individual believer and the Church catholic is the "glorified humanity of Christ crucified, resurrected and ascended." We continue to honor and praise God for the creative genius of gender differentiation (that is, for humanity constituted as male and female), yet recognize that gender is no longer *the* defining characteristic of one's identity, individual or communal, in Christ. In fact, the differentiated reciprocity of associated genders discloses the divine plan of the created order as an ontological reality comparable to the diversified unity of the one *body of Christ*.

The affirmation that Christ is center goes beyond what has already been stated and removes from the table any notion of the church as some form of voluntary organization or democratically run institution, whether at the local level or that of the wider church. Acknowledging Christ as center endorses both the organic reality of church as dependent on the differentiating presence of Christ, which constitutes *church as church*, while at the same time reaffirms the church's accountability to him who is Head and Lord. The church is not *church* so long as she functions under the illusion that she is democratically constituted and capable of discharging her several responsibilities, and even restructuring her identity, without reference to him who is both Head and Lord. Although he was addressing the issue of ministerial authority in the church, Nevin's admonition is still pertinent to the point at issue:

> The people have just as little right here as parliament and kings to shape the Church to their own ends, or take the creation of ministry into their own hands. The fond notion which some have of a republican or democratic order in Christianity, by which the popular vote, or the will of any mass or majority of (people), shall be regarded sufficient to originate or bring to an end the sacred office wherever it may be thought proper, and even to create, if

need seem, a new Church, as they dare to prostitute the glorious name, for its service and use—is just as removed from the proper truth of the gospel as any other that could well be applied to the subject.[16]

To the degree that the UCC as a conciliar fellowship seeks to promote a conciliar identity, the church demonstrates a proleptic realization of the fulfillment of the unity Christ desires and the genuineness of its own ecclesiological self-understanding as a *united* and *uniting* church.

---

16. Ibid., 113.

5

National Setting

As previously stated, the UCC came into existence in 1957 after a long and often labored series of conversations between representatives of two streams of Protestantism whose roots date back to the sixteenth and seventeenth centuries: the Evangelical and Reformed Church and the Congregational Christian Churches. The intent of the merger, or more accurately *covenantal* agreement, was to be and become a *united* and *uniting* church. The creation of this conciliar fellowship was the result of a series of bilateral dialogues in the attempt to achieve initial congruence.

A CHURCH UNITED AND UNITING

In his book, *The Shaping of the United Church of Christ*, Louis Gunnemann describes the essential stages in the process of creating the UCC:

> The United Church of Christ began its existence with a formidable vision: the UCC would be the stimulus for a generation of mergers among U.S. Protestants. If it did not become the chief inspiration, surely it would participate eagerly in all such ventures. The uniting Synod shaped that vision, first by deliberately choosing a name, United Church of Christ, free from doctrinal controversy and prior denominational ownership. No mere name could ever be allowed to impede additional mergers. The vision was shaped, second, when the motto "United and Uniting" was adopted to express the fundamental UCC ecumenical hope. This vision was shaped, third, with the adoption by the 1959 Synod of Paragraph 1 of the Preamble to the UCC Constitution, stating forthrightly that the UCC ecumenical vocation is to express "more fully the oneness with Christ." One defining characteristic of the UCC is its ecumenical commitment, expressed and shaped for all time by these major decisions regarding its name, motto, and vocation.[1]

---

1. Gunnemann, *Shaping of the United Church of Christ*, 208–9.

The three major foci Gunnemann describes so clearly justify my principle goal. Persistent debate over social issues that are politically and theologically charged has contributed to a loss of our church's essential focus among many members of the UCC. Like other church bodies, we have experienced a deepening polarization among members and member churches of the UCC and between the UCC and other churches in the ecumenical movement. We have drifted far from the defining vision-and-vocation of 1957, weakening the advance of the ecumenical cause at a grassroots level.

In what is arguably a piece of prophetic insight, lawyer and lay theologian William Stringfellow once wrote:

> Among American Protestants, the Reformation principle of dissent and of the integrity of the relationship between God and [humanity] was transmuted into a radical individualism which made each [hu]man the author of his [or her] own religion. For more than a century and a half, Protestantism has nurtured this notion of autonomous and personal religiosity, and this notion, more than any other single factor, explains the grotesque division, separation, and segregation of the Church in the United States and the stifling religious ethos in which Christians in America find themselves today.[2]

The purpose of Stringfellow's writing is not to direct attention to ecumenical issues. His concern is with the relationship between

2. Stringfellow, *Public and Private Faith*, 19. In order to place Stringfellow's comment in its proper context, one must recall that the Catholic Church entered the ecumenical effort with the conciliar *Decree on Ecumenism*, which was issued on November 21, 1964! There have been significant advances in ecumenicity in the period since Stringfellow made his critical observation, including COCU and the publication of *Baptism, Eucharist, and Ministry*, efforts that have demonstrated the unity we share and hold promise for the furtherance of other visible forms of unity. Writing in 1967, Bernard Lambert observed: "In the United States, so far, the prevailing form of ecumenism has been co-operative in character. American Protestant Christianity has attained powerful and distinct means of expression; it is co-operative, social, missionary, eager to speak to every department of human life." Lambert, *Ecumenism: Theology and History*, 113. Lambert's comment highlights another development in ecumenicity; often the questions of faith and order have been left in the background, and the main emphasis has been placed on those of faith and work, or on the witness, through life and work, to the saving power of Christ at work in society. One could hypothesize that Stringfellow may have applauded such a shift in focus, and in particular among those American Protestant churches in which "personal religiosity" had corrupted the churches. See Lambert, *Ecumenism: Theology and History*, chapter 3 for a full description of the transition in focus within the ecumenical movement.

the privatization of religious convictions and the need for the church (in North America) to address public issues from the vantage point of the gospel mandate; nonetheless, his observation is relevant to our purpose. Prolonged and acrimonious debate over controversial issues has often ended in church members defining themselves by reference to the limited attributes and theological categories of their individual convictions on public policy. In this light, Stringfellow issues an even more cogent warning:

> Insofar as American Protestantism begins . . . in the ecumenical discussions with Roman Catholics and Orthodox and Anglican Christians, to remember something of the corporate existence of the Church, something of the Oneness and Holiness of the Body of Christ, it must necessarily and inevitably abandon its historic association—its guilty association—with the radical individualism which has so dominated its thought and organization and way of life in the United States.[3]

Such issues and recurring debate do not represent the ecclesial concerns of the representatives involved in negotiating the union that first formed the UCC. These ecumenical conversations proved foundational to the *Basis of Union* adopted in 1948–49. This document defined the principles and tasks of the undivided church as well as annunciating the newly formed community's ecumenical commitment as an expression of faithful obedience to the will of Christ. As stated in the preamble to that document:

> We, the regularly constituted representatives of the Congregational Christian Churches and of the Evangelical and Reformed Church, *moved by the conviction that we are united in spirit and purpose and are in agreement on the substance of the Christian faith and the essential character of the Christian life;*

Affirming devotion to the one God, the Father of our Lord Jesus Christ, and our membership in the holy Catholic Church, which is greater than any single Church and than all the Churches together;

Believing that denominations exist not for themselves but as parts of that Church, within which each denomination is to live and labor, and if need be, die; and confronting the divisions and hostilities of our world, and hearing with a deepened sense of responsibility the prayer of our Lord "that they may all be one;"

---

3. Ibid., 31.

Do now declare ourselves to be one body, and do set forth the following articles of agreement as the basis of our life, fellowship, witness, and proclamation of the Gospel to all nations.[4]

Throughout its relatively brief history, the UCC has prided itself as an experiment in ecumenicity with the expressed desire to pursue relationships of shared mission and ministry with other confessional bodies. Charles Shelby Rooks asserts that "the UCC ecumenical commitment [has been] shaped annually by a broad spectrum of church unity discussions in which it was heavily involved." Writing in 1999, he asserted that after four decades of existence "the UCC ecumenical vision is as strong as it has ever been." He supplies a list of what he calls "ecumenical episodes" in the years since 1957 as evidence for his claim, including:

- Adoption of a Covenant of Mission and Faith between the UCC and the Evangelical Church of the Union in Germany . . .
- Creation of an ecumenical partnership between the UCC and the Christian Church (Disciples of Christ) . . .
- Participation in the Lutheran-Reformed Dialogue which led to the adoption of the resolution "Full Communion with the Evangelical Lutheran Church in America, the Presbyterian Church (USA) and the Reformed Church in America" by the 1997 General Synod
- Membership in the World Alliance of Reformed Churches, the International Council of Congregational Churches, the World Council of Churches, and the National Council of Churches in the USA
- The development of important UCC/Partner Church relationships with churches around the world under the policies and initiatives of the United Church Board for World Ministries after approval by the General Synod[5]

THE LOCAL SETTING

I too would credit the UCC with the advances listed above; however, it is my contention that the UCC has failed to engage the laity in ongoing ecumenical efforts. The selection listed above demonstrates the national

---

4. Gunnemann, *United and Uniting*, 23, 26. (Emphasis mine.)
5. Gunnemann, *Shaping of the United Church of Christ*, 211–12.

church's continuing interest in and active pursuit of an ecumenical agenda. But the vision-and-vocation—central to the initial formation and theological thrust of the UCC—has *not* made a significant impact on members of the local congregation. Ecumenicity has had little or no effect on the worldview of local church members. If this ecumenical distinction, so crucial to our church's ecclesial self-understanding from its inception, does not incite identity formation at the grassroots level, then the ongoing promotion of the original ecumenical vision-and-vocation is impoverished. The lively participation of local church members in any ecumenical effort is, without question, indispensable to the movement toward greater unity.[6]

The availability of resources from the antecedent traditions of the UCC has in many ways been a tool for the enrichment of the entire church. Yet the contribution each tradition makes to our ecumenical vision-and-vocation, as well as the contribution made to the formation of an ecclesial identity, has seldom been made clear to members of the local congregation. In pastoral experience, I have found that this has led to deepening confusion and a sense of frustration among members of the local congregation.

Seldom if ever are members of the local congregation challenged to learn more about the richness of the antecedent traditions of the UCC; they focus instead on the particulars of their own congregation's theological heritage and ecclesiological history.[7] Ecumenist Douglas Horton is attributed with having said that "we shall continue to be frustrated from making the kind of contribution we could make to the ecumenical understanding of the church until we are prepared to give as much serious study to our constituent ecclesiologies as Roman Catholics, Anglo-Catholics, Lutherans, or Baptists are prepared to give to their own."[8]

---

6. "So long as local churches do not see themselves as *agents* of unity, division will not be seen as a matter that touches them. The congregation down the street must be a matter of concern, not only on special occasions or in a purely formal way, but as an element in the regular ordering of the internal life of the local church." Braaten and Jenson, *In One Body*, 51.

7. In his book *Freedom with Order*, Robert S. Paul writes: "I fear that one of the reasons we have failed to make the kind of ecumenical impact that we should have made has been our failure to take our traditions with due seriousness. As a result our 'ecumenism' has seemed to be simply a matter of practical expediency or union for the sake of being bigger, whereas originally it arose out of our essential theology: that is, it arose originally out of our fundamental belief about God, about God's good news in Jesus Christ, and about the church's mission." Paul, *Freedom with Order*, 40.

8. Ibid.

There is far more at issue than clarification of what it means to be a member of the UCC. The question of identity goes directly to the heart of how church can be *church*, dealing with some the most pressing theological and critical social issues facing the church.[9] In the absence of any clear understanding of what it means to belong to a conciliar fellowship, one wonders how contributing to such deliberations will genuinely reflect commitment to the catholicity and unity of the church.

Many members of the local congregation—and not a few clergy—retreat to their own historical and theological heritage, not so much as a resource to help them address controversial issues, but as a safeguard against being labeled "liberal" or "conservative." With alarming frequency local congregations of the UCC, in disagreement with stated pronouncements of the national church, have withdrawn from this conciliar fellowship as though the covenant were little more than a "club" membership terminated at will. In such contentious matters, neither side seems to possess the requisite *spiritus humilis* to practice the necessary *metanoia* that would make possible reconciliation and a return to the central focus of a conciliar fellowship—seeking to bring about visible unity, not engineer deeper fractures in Christian fellowship!

As a participant in a consultation on the dilemma of UCC polity and identity sponsored by the Board for Homeland Ministries, held in 1979, Robert S. Paul commented:

> If the ecumenical vision that inspired our original union remains a major objective of our church, then the principle of catholicity, inclusiveness, is vital to that goal, and it also has a curious effect on the problem of our present self-identity . . . a church that maintains the ecumenical goal cannot be other than a community of faith that seeks catholicity in the fullest sense. The United Church of Christ has little reason for separated existence today, unless, *in the kind of church it tries to be*, it points all churches to the God of the biblical revelation who alone brings the One, Holy, Catholic, and Apostolic Church into being.[10]

---

9. A sampling of the issues would include: biblical authority, standards of ordination, abortion, same-sex unions, communing children, and stewardship of creation.

10. Paul, *Freedom with Order*, 84–85.

AUTONOMY REVISITED

As I mentioned in a previous chapter, many members in the local congregation do not understand the polity of the UCC in general and the concept of congregational autonomy in particular. Frequently, this term, rich with theological and covenantal intent, is perceived to mean little more than freedom from the constraints of some external authority. This misconception has often led both members and congregations to feel little or no sense of obligation to the wider church and to the Church catholic. It has also become commonplace for the assertion of autonomy to be used to justify further divisions, as individual churches sever ties to the UCC in order to become independent, reclaiming allegiance to a truncated version of an antecedent tradition, or claiming to be "Reformed" with no connection whatsoever to the theological convictions of the historical Reformed family.

The tragic occurrence in which churches decide to sever relations with the UCC has been particularly painful in the last two decades. Congregations first withdraw financial support of the UCC's wider mission, but eventually and for many, separation is inevitable. The formation of conciliar identity would not ensure that congregants are less likely to support such separation. However, congregants may come to appreciate autonomy as a theological term, Christ centered and bounded by covenantal obligations, and be disinclined to rush to judgment regarding separation from the wider church. They may also recognize the nurturing of unity as *obligatory* and not optional.

The *Basis of Union*, as an invaluable resource, can remind local church members that "unity in Christ leaves no room for any autonomy of tradition, culture, ethnicity, race, class, sex, political (or anything else that we call 'Christian pluralism') by which we justify our divisions."[11] Gunnemann offer this trenchant comment:

> It is, then, the *autonomy* of diverse elements of identity that must be challenged and surrendered in a united church. Absolutizing (asserting autonomy) of individual freedom and private judgment may elevate diversity but preclude the possibility of exhibiting the unity of the Body of Christ. The apostle Paul's clear statement about this in 1 Corinthians and in his letter to the Ephesians draw the line of limitation around the place of diversity. There is "one Lord, one faith, one baptism, one God." The experience of

---

11. Gunnemann, *United and Uniting*, 48.

that oneness may be diverse, but the identifying mark is *oneness*, not diversity.¹²

My stated interest is the endorsement of conciliar identity among members of the local congregation, yet this in no way precludes concern for those members in the national church who struggle with the issue of identity. It is interesting to note how frequently letters to the editor of the UCC's now discontinued national newspaper (*United Church News*) were written from the vantage point of the writer's "private judgment," with little or no evidence given of any awareness of how this assertion of individual freedom merely reinforces the stereotypical image of our church as having little unification, harmony, or genuine ecumenicity¹³ among members of the local congregation.

Gunneman's observation that the identifying mark of the UCC is "*oneness*, not diversity" simply flies in the face of perspectives being promoted by the national offices of the UCC and through questionable techniques for attracting new members to the church. Promotional programs such as the "God is still speaking" effort tend to reinforce the element of "diversity" as representative of the *whole* of the UCC and fail to endorse and promote the greater ecumenical heritage of the church. As I stated previously, the use of the comma may be a clever technique for promotional purposes, but I would contend that it is as careless as it is clever, in that it misrepresents the heart and soul of the UCC as a conciliar body accountable to the Church catholic and her ecumenical partners in dialog. "Oneness" is endangered when we ignore just how offensive our ecumenical partners find such moves as the replacement of the Cross of Victory with a punctuation mark of comedic origin!

---

12. Ibid., 49.

13. In the December 2003 issue of the *United Church News*, there was an article entitled "Who do they say that we are?" in which members representative of a variety of church traditions offered "some constructive criticism about our denomination's identity." It is sobering to read the comments and see how others define our church and the characteristics attributed to our identity. There are exceptionally few references to the ecumenical character of the UCC, with far more emphases placed on "open, liberal, socially active, and easy-going." My point is simply this: were members of the local church more faithfully engaged in the ecumenical vision-and-vocation with which the UCC began, and were they better educated in the characteristics of a *conciliar identity*, there would most likely be a much clearer projection of who we are to the general public and to the wider church. J. Bennett Guess, "Who do they say that we are?" *United Church News*, 19, no. 10 (December 2003) A8–A9.

Time and again I have been reminded by lay people that such promotional gimmicks are an affront to the church they have grown to love and the theological richness they have long held to be essential to their identity as disciples of Christ. Even for those—and they are the majority—who are unable to articulate, with precision, the elements of that same theological heritage, there is an expressed concern that such promotional publicity stunts merely cast the whole of the UCC in a bad light, making it increasingly difficult for them to defend against those who perceive the UCC as little more than a body of "liberal" Christians with little or no regard for the traditions of the Christian faith. Interestingly, the "reformation" of the church has always come from the "bottom-up" rather than from the "top-down"!

6

Reflections: Pastoral and Theological

THE FOLLOWING CHAPTER OFFERS theological and pastoral reflections foundational to the development of my argument. Beginning with general observations, I then present a concise account of the terms and metaphors that support of my contention. A discussion of biblical and theological idioms (for example, *covenant*) is followed by remarks on the use of terms like *place* and *home*, principally for their metaphorical value in clarifying one of the aims of my overall design.

There is an indisputable link between the content of beliefs held and the Christian practices in which one is equipped to participate. Amy Platinga Pauw persuasively argues that "weakly held or inconsistent beliefs are a barrier to good practice. Though the epistemic capital of a religious community can carry its doubting and theologically disinclined members along for a considerable time, the long-term viability of a community demands efforts at consistency between beliefs and practice."[1]

Serene Jones has written that "beliefs are often determined by (and therefore don't simply determine) the specificity of the practices that live within and through them."[2] Dallas Willard writes: "In our day learners usually think of themselves as containers of some sort, with a purely passive space to be filled by the information the teacher possesses and wishes to transfer. We then 'test' the students to see if they 'got it' by checking whether they can *reproduce* it in language rather than watching how they live."[3] My concern is to fortify both ecumenically based beliefs and the associated practices in a reciprocity that is mutually reinforcing.

---

1. This is but a small portion of a much more complex argument: Pauw, "Attending the Gaps," *Practicing Theology*, 33–48.
2. Serene Jones, "Graced Practices," 76.
3. Willard, *Divine Conspiracy*, 112–13.

My aim is similar to what Willard argues was common among teachers in the time of Jesus. Describing the method Jesus might have employed, Willard contends that he most likely used the form established among teachers in his own cultural setting where "the aim of the popular teacher . . . was not to impart information, but to make significant change in the lives of the hearers. Of course that may require information transfer, but it is a peculiarly modern notion that the aim of teaching is to bring things that may have no effect at all on their lives."[4]

Kathryn Tanner cautions that "in order to figure out how to go on, one must, with some measure of reflective exertion, figure out the meaning of what one has been doing, why one does it, and what it implies—in particular, how it hangs together (or fails to hang together) with the rest of what one believes and does. Because of their ambiguities, inconsistencies, and open-endedness, practices, in short, do not run by automatic or mechanical routine but through at best quasi-reflective or deliberate effort to figure out what to do next, how to proceed."[5]

I would argue for nurturing the kind of theological reflection and critical engagement that is essential to internalizing the characteristics basic to the formation of conciliar identity and the capacity to further ecumenical initiatives at the local level. In an insightful article, "Identity and Ecumenicity," Piet J. Naudé observes:

> One of the perennial problems in the ecumenical movement is the strained relation between churches' self-understanding and the aim "to call the churches to the goal of visible unity in one faith and in common life in Christ." The problem may be restated . . . as that between (ecclesial) identity and (holy) communion. The great ecumenical theologian Geoffery Wainright declares: "At stake in the understanding of unity and schism, of continuity and discontinuity, of integrity and fragmentation, is precisely the *identity of the church* and therewith the nature and substance of truth and the conditions of its *authoritative expression*.[6]

In his subtitle ("How Do We Deal Theologically with So-Called 'Nontheological' Factors?"), Naudé indicates that he focuses on nontheological factors contributing to the creation of obstacles in the ecumenical movement, in both bilateral and multilateral conversations. He

---

4. Ibid., 112.
5. Tanner, "Theological Reflection," 232.
6. Naudé, "Identity and Ecumenicity," 435–36.

refers to factors "like geography, language, culture, and in particular, history" as well as "nationality, race, class, and self-preservation."[7] Such nontheological factors have impeded ecumenicity. Naudé states that divided churches today are "in a state of powerful inner contradiction," where years ago "they greeted the ecumenical era with enthusiasm . . . the situation has changed. Today the churches stress their own identity and tradition."[8]

While the UCC has made significant strides in pursuit of an ecumenical vision, it is nonetheless true that for members at the level of the local congregation there remain theological and nontheological factors contributing to a real void in the capacity to comprehend, embrace, celebrate, and participate in the church's ecumenical vision-and-vocation. Naudé also argues that "the process of the ecumenical movement has indeed stumbled over [a] negative flight into an isolationist 'identity,'"[9] which is often the case in local settings of the UCC, where too often members identify their commitments in relation to the history of their own congregation and indigenous traditions.

The tendency to retreat into an isolationist identity or to define one's self by reference to stereotypical categories (for example, liberal, conservative, or evangelical) deepens at the local level, as individuals and churches face off on hot-button issues like abortion or same-sex relationships. Again Naudé is helpful when he states that "the approach to understanding the reasons for both church divisions and church union from social sources must be welcomed as an important facet of contextual analysis crucial to theology. It does assist the theologian to understand the historical, economic, and cultural factors at play in the struggle for the visible unity of the local (regional) and universal church. *But these insights must be interpreted theologically to make a lasting impact on bilateral and multilateral dialogues.*"[10] There are any number of factors contributing to (what we would call) an unconventional Christian identity or, in even more pregnant terms, a deviant Christian identity, among many in the UCC. For many in the local congregation, identity is grounded in either culturally informed patterns of belief or an amalgam of beliefs from a culturally informed and generalized spirituality. A

7. Ibid., 436.
8. Ibid.
9. Ibid.
10. Ibid., 439.

crisis of Christian identity can also be witnessed among members of the wider Christian community and is therefore an ecumenical and shared concern;[11] yet my primary concern is with membership identity in the local setting of the UCC.

The crisis of identity might also be attributed to postmodern culture, in which religion and religious beliefs are appreciated principally for their pragmatic value and not so much for the way in which they call into question or even alter one's identity.[12] Or the crisis can be credited to an enculturation of Christian faith (at least on the North American continent) in which beliefs and associated practices are informed and shaped more by the current fascination with pluralism and relativism than by the more orthodox creedal and confessional beliefs of the Church catholic.[13]

Each and all of these factors together have contributed to the current crisis in Christian identity generally, exasperating Christian identity among many in the local setting of the UCC more particularly. In *The Shaping of the United Church of Christ*, Gunnemann states that

> for many people in major American denominations "the experience of religious faith" had no transcendent referent at all; the experience was in the realm of interpersonal relationships. To find religious identity in "loving and caring" relationships did not nec-

11. Writing from the perspective of a Reformed theologian, and more particularly as a member of the Presbyterian Church (USA), P. Mark Achtemeier offers a very helpful description of those areas of ecclesiological and theological concern in which "American Protestantism" in general (and the implied Christian identity) needs to be corrected. He sites "discipleship, authority, mission, and unity," as among the most essential areas to be addressed. Achtemeier, "*Union with Christ* Doctrine," 336–45.

12. I am in full agreement with Naudé when he concludes that "nontheological/social factors in their negative determination of identity (neurosis in therapeutic terms; righteousness through the flesh in biblical terms) are only 'overcome' via a radical reorientation to Christ (re-symbolization in therapeutic terms; conversion in biblical terms) that works a new self-understanding in the light of Christ's second coming (re-interpretation in therapeutic terms; expectation in biblical terms)." Naudé, "Identity and Ecumenicity," 448.

13. In what is a superb analysis of the current situation, Lesslie Newbigin in *The Gospel in a Pluralist Society* states the case succinctly, with tongue-in-cheek: "What matters is not the factual content of faith claims but the sincerity with which they are held. They are matters not of public knowledge but of personal faith. Knowing is one thing, and the schools are there to see that everyone knows what we all need to know about the real facts. Believing is something else, that is, it is a personal matter for each individual. Each of us should have a personal faith of our own." Newbigin, *Gospel in a Pluralist Society*, 26.

essarily require a particular religious community or a particular faith in a transcendent deity. Thus, the church as a community of faith lost its meaning for many people. Other communities and other relationships supplanted the church in the lives of people who, in a society of pluralistic value, had many options.[14]

While its first publication was in 1977, Gunnemann's book has not lost its relevance or applicability.

In a more contemporary context, John H. Thomas, former general minister and president of the UCC, claims that the church in the twenty-first century faces similar issues to those described by Gunnemann. Thomas writes that "a primary challenge for religious institutions will be learning to respond to this spiritual quest culture, providing communities of commitment, engagement, and tradition where these spiritual consumers become celebrants of a Gospel that transcends traditions but is always embodied by them. Central to this challenge is discerning what role, if any, those inherited ecclesial traditions will play in this response."[15]

Furthermore, Thomas argues that our ecumenical vision-and-vocation could serve to persuade the local church "to think critically about identities that have been used arrogantly and at times abusively to denote distinctiveness over against others and to discover instead deeper or transcending commonalities in converging understandings of the central doctrines and practices of the faith."[16]

My intention in this book is not to flatten out the richness and diversity of expressions of Christian faith. Rather, I want to create an ecumenical environment where members of the UCC can gain a deeper appreciation of that same diversity while obtaining clarity regarding their own identity as conciliar Christians. Diversity of faith-expression adds to the richness of our ecumenical vision.

Thomas is right to claim that differences are to be seen "as gifts to be shared, rather than as the building blocks of clear boundaries," so that "denominations begin to take on a changing vocation."[17] Pluralism is not thought of purely in negative terms, as though of little value. It is not so much living in a pluralistic environment, as it is the response of the church (both the local and wider church) to pluralism that proves

14. Gunnemann, *Shaping of the United Church of Christ*, 105–6.
15. Thomas, "Salt that Seasons."
16. Ibid.
17. Ibid.

problematic. Daniel Migliore has written: "On the positive side, pluralism espouses respect for individuality, particularity, and difference, and resists the drive toward total control and homogenization of life by dominant cultures, ideologies, and political powers. On the negative side, pluralism can be debilitating and disintegrative. A pluralist society completely indifferent to common beliefs, norms, and values is a society at grave risk."[18]

Migliore delineates some of the more common responses to pluralism in the life of the church. On the one hand, the church has responded with an unhealthy fixation on the need to grow local membership in order to maintain (a perceived) dominance over other forms of religious expression, or other Christian confessions. On the other hand, the church has often chosen to withdraw from the social context and its perceived threat, establishing an isolationist mentality among its members. As a third alternative, the church has chosen accommodation with the prevailing culture rather than risk the loss of members whose lives are shaped by a plurality of cultural convictions.[19] Migliore recommends his own response informed by the doctrine of the triune God: "In a pluralist context where the reality of community is elusive and the quest for community acute, the church must dare to speak concretely and specifically about what God has done to establish new community in Jesus Christ by the power of the Spirit. In the light of the gospel, human community has its basis and promise in the life and activity of the triune God."[20]

The concept of the church as a communion conditionally disclosing the inner life of the triune God has become a common theme among ecumenists. Where the church reveals otherness and difference and yet manifests ecumenical oneness, the richness of the triune God, in the unity of eternal being, is honored as the source and sustaining power of the church's life. We turn once again to the petition of our Lord's high priestly prayer as found in John 17: "I ask not only on behalf of these, but also on behalf of those who will believe in me through their word, that they may all be one. As you, Father, are in me and I am in you, may

---

18. Migliore, "The Communion of the Triune God," 141.

19. Ibid., 142.

20. Ibid. See also footnote 9 in the same essay in which (referencing an article in the same volume, but authored by Ulrich Körtner) Migliore recommends that one not make a too facile move from reference to the inner life of the triune God to the reality of the church as human community. One needs to be very careful not to give the impression of sponsoring some form of idealistic ecclesiology!

they also be in us, so that the world may believe that you sent me. The glory that you have given me I have given them, so that they may be one, as we are one, I in them and you in me, that they may be completely one, so that the world may know that you have sent me and have loved them even as you have loved me" (John 17:20–23). In this portion of his prayer, our Lord has made it abundantly clear that there is a direct correlation between the hypostatic unity of his being as the Christ and Son of God, the internal unity of the triune life, the unity to be made manifest in the community of faith, and the veracity of the proclaimed word to a disjointed and divisive world. We are not speaking here of the achievement of a perfected state of "oneness" in the Church catholic, but of the necessity for the church—in all her diversity—to seek greater visible unity in faithful response to the plaintive prayer of her Lord and Savior. To this degree, ecumenicity must be far more than another programmatic effort of the churches; rather, Christians in every church must embrace ecumenicity as an imperative of Christ on their knees before the Father!

Yet the church suffers from the divisions caused by disobedience and sin. The Reformed heritage speaks of the eschatological reserve: while the church celebrates and seeks to further the unity it has in Christ, it also acknowledges that its communion is provisional. Fragmentation and failure are not necessarily inevitable. Under the present condition of *simul justus et peccator*,[21] sin will continue to disrupt the church's present communion and harmony, and all efforts to achieve unity. Until the advent of the triune God's kingdom and the consummation of God's

---

21. Although he includes a rather terse definition of the term, Douglas John Hall's commentary on the "fundamental biblical dialectic of the individual and the community" is helpful: "It has been very difficult, it would seem, for the church throughout the centuries to appropriate this dialectic. The most rudimentary reasons for that difficulty lie, of course, in the mystery of human sin: the rebellious and ubiquitous 'I' continues to assert itself long after it has experienced the grace of justification! *Simul justus et peccator* (at the same time justified and sinner—Luther). But the social status of the church can also affect this issue. When the structures of the church mirror the structures of a hierarchically arranged society, for example, as they have done throughout the history of Christianity, they provide the external circumstances favorable to egoistic self-assertion in the Christian community, and thus militate against the realization of the new and grace-given possibilities to which, for example, Paul is alluding in his metaphor of the body of Christ (*sōma Christou/corpus Christi*). Is it not possible that, as the church enters the quite different sociological situation which pertains at 'the end of the Constantinian era,' it could more fully realize the meaning of reconciliation and human communion in its own life?" Hall, *Thinking the Faith*, 292.

redemptive plan for the church and for the whole of the world, this is the reality of both church and world. Acknowledgement of this reality will prohibit the church from unrealistic expectations, while at the same time providing continuity in commitment to the pursuit of visible unity as an expression of our having embraced and invested in the coming kingdom and the promised consummation of all things, when even Christ will hand over all to the Father so that God will be "all-in-all." After all, one cannot invest in that which one does not believe; should we fail to believe that the pursuit of visible unity is *at the core* of our Christian gospel and mission, we might find that the world will disbelieve that genuine harmony and the unity that overcomes division can ever be fully realized. We must learn to hold in creative tension the *simul justus et peccator* and the dynamism of a promised future in which God will fulfill all things in a unity unparalleled at present.

7

Semper Reformanda

The Holy Spirit upholds our bond of unity in Christ and also upholds the reconciliation of all things beginning with the household of faith (Eph 2:19–22). In a situation of "already" and "not yet," the church acknowledges "that all confessional statements and theologies this side of the promised reign of God are *semper reformanda*."[1] The *ecclesia reformata secundum verbi Dei semper reformanda*[2] remains a significant characteristic of Reformed ecclesiology.[3] The Church catholic, as a communal agent and not merely any one or more of the constituting members, is called by God to repentance and reformation in the light of God's Word and under the auspices of the Holy Spirit. Both the desire for reformation and the actuality of transformation are products of God's prior action in the Holy Spirit; both represent the transcendent dimension to my proposal.

Repentance and renewal (a variation on reformation and transformation) are also theological themes of vital interest to the ecumenical movement.[4] In their introductory article to the book entitled *Reformed Theology: Identity and Ecumenicity*, Alston and Welker write:

1. Migliore, "Communion of the Triune God," 145.

2. Guder writes: "That phrase *ecclesia reformata secundum verbi Dei semper reformanda*, is used a great deal in North Atlantic Reformed circles these days, probably because of the crisis in which most of these churches find themselves. It is indeed a work of God's Spirit when we recognize that under the guidance of the Word of God the church must constantly experience re-shaping, re-forming." Guder, *Continuing Conversion of the Church*, 150.

3. George W. Stroup argues that the phrase has often been mistranslated as "the church reformed, always reforming," and should more accurately be rendered " 'the church reformed, always being reformed' by the Word of God," as the "mistranslation erroneously suggests that it is the church rather than the sovereign God who is the agent of transformation." Stroup, "Reformed Identity," 261.

4. Michael Kinnamon offers a compelling description of the reasons why repen-

> If the "ecclesia reformata et semper reformanda" is to be true to its sources and its calling, it must live in constant search of truth, it must be ready to repent and learn, and it must be prepared to bear witness and to give account, time and again, for its theological convictions and certainties. It lives . . . continually testing its cherished customs and convictions on the way from individual and communal certainties to the fuller disclosure of truth.[5]

Both *semper reformanda* and repentance—as a movement toward renewal—play a role in the formation of a conciliar identity as the willingness to acknowledge the need for repentance and reliance upon God, who alone is the source of forgiveness, restoration, and renewal in the church. Recognizing God alone as the "author and finisher" of this process of reformation or renewal, whether one favors the language of "*semper reformanda*" or "repentance," maintains a transcendent and therefore transformational dimension to the formation of conciliar identity. These concepts are not optional in reclaiming the originating vision-and-vocation of the UCC; as Michael Kinnamon has written, "ecumenism requires: (1) repentance for the ways we have borne witness against our neighbors as well as false witness against the unity that is ours in Christ, and (2) conversion to a new way of seeing ourselves and others."[6]

In his article entitled "Paradox Catholicity," Ulrich Körtner argues that it is "part of the irresolvable ambivalence of the church that every effort for visible unity, no matter in what shape, leads to new problems of polarization and separation . . . this provisional characteristic is the reality of the church; the expressed desire to pursue unity as well as action taken in that direction are denied the possibility of being seen as the final

---

tance is a vital theme in all ecumenical encounters when he writes: "The one church in Christ, which is God's gift sustained by the Holy Spirit, may be without spot or wrinkle. The historical churches, however, filled with sinful persons, have fought one another for worldly advantage, have acted like competing corporations instead of independent parts of a single body, have allowed secondary loyalties to override their shared commitment to Christ. How can the churches possibly speak of reconciliation or communion without confessing these sins to God and one another? There have been times when commitment to the gospel truth has led Christians to break fellowship with others who claim Christ's name. Many divisions, however, have less noble roots: personal animosities, desire for power, fear of otherness. How can churches possibly speak of unity without a public resolve to live, with God's help, in a different way?" Kinnamon, *Vision of the Ecumenical Movement*, 68.

5. Alston and Welker, introduction to *Reformed Theology*, x.
6. Kinnamon, *Vision of the Ecumenical Movement*, 65.

solution to separation."⁷ This condition mandates dependence upon the grace and mercy of God, requiring acts of repentance in anticipation of renewal. Körtner offers the "sign of the cross of Christ" as the symbol of both judgment and grace, contributing to an ecumenical theology that is grounded in the redemptive suffering of Christ "including the suffering of ecclesiastical separations."⁸

Körtner makes reference to John Williamson Nevin, one of the proponents of the Mercersburg theology, an expression of the Reformed confession in the United States and still evident in some circles of the UCC.⁹ Nevin is quoted as having argued that "Jesus intervened in his praying for the unity of the church. If this was the spirit of Christ, then the spirit of the church can only convene with him. The whole church sighs in her fragmentation, as if Christ himself had been affected by the separation and could not find peace until the unnatural deed of violence had come to its end."¹⁰ In light of such an understanding of Christ's suffering and cross Körtner wishes to redefine the "*semper reformanda*":

> Whenever plurality is described in a one-sided fashion as an essential feature of all communities, one needs to be reminded that through the word of reconciliation God not only accepts this ecclesiastical plurality but at the same time places it under his judgment. The ambivalence of plurality, i.e., the unity of identity and difference, is that it not only signifies legitimate diversity but also sinful separation. True reconciliation does not intend mere reciprocal acceptance, but reciprocal atonement and renewal.¹¹

Körtner concludes his discussion by commending the practical outcome of such reciprocal reconciliation as "a simultaneous acceptance and transformation of the historically grown denominational identities,"

---

7. Körtner, "Paradox Catholicity," 98–411.

8. Ibid., 410.

9. The Mercersburg Society continues to meet annually, publishes its own theological journal, the *Mercersburg Review*, and continues to explore the ecumenical themes and catholic characteristics of the theological expressions of such guiding lights as John Williamson Nevin and Philip Schaff. While the impact of the research and publications of this society have not made a substantial impact on the national church (UCC), its influence can be felt more directly in such reform movements as "Confessing Christ." In another essay, I have argued for the contributions Mercersburg theology can make to the formation of an "ecumenical identity" (a variation on the theme extended in this essay). Walsh, "One Model of Christian Identity," 50–62.

10. Körtner, "Paradox Catholicity," 410.

11. Ibid., 410–11.

which can only be accomplished by those who recognize that "any reconciled diversity can only be obtained at the price of the 'dying to Christ,' which makes denominational identities not only relative, but possibly transforms them."[12] During the verbal defense of my thesis, which is the basis of this book, one of my professors questioned aloud whether, in fact, I was promoting and prepared to see the "death" of denominations, to which I replied in the affirmative. It is not some melancholic disapproval of denominations that led to this conviction, but the suspicion that genuine "repentance" may not be possible if we continue to maintain unhealthy investiture in denominational differences, primarily because we fear what will be demanded of *us* should we no longer have the safety of organizational structures!

Körtner's proposal is compelling on a number of levels—among them is his realistic appraisal of what can be accomplished, even among the most committed ecumenical partners, and his interpretation of *"semper reformanda"* as shaped by a theology of suffering (more accurately, Christ's suffering and crucifixion). Furthermore, he contends that a result of reciprocal reconciliation will be the "transformation of denominational bodies." Körtner provides balance; he suggests a corrective against the tendency to idealize either ecumenicity or ecclesiology, imparting a theological rationale for the formation of conciliar identity sufficiently bounded by the realism of Christ's cross on one side and the promise of Christ's resurrection and return in glory on the other.

A transition in theological conceptualization can now be made from this series of reflections on the *semper reformanda* of the Reformed tradition to the concept of covenant as a term with theological specificity in the history of the UCC and its antecedent traditions. This paradigm shift does not neglect the connection between the *semper reformanda* and repentance, which I have already discussed; the concept of covenant—adequately defined and characterized—is the relational dynamic in which the stated themes are enacted. Or in more descriptive language, *semper reformanda* and repentance are presupposed in the concept of covenant and the covenant is sustained and enriched by the enactment of both repentance and *semper reformanda*. I will first draw some broad strokes of definition and then narrow my focus to the importance covenant has for my argument.

---

12. Ibid., 411.

COVENANT IN HISTORICAL PERSPECTIVE

George W. Stroup contends that it is "common procedure in ecumenical conversations [to] attempt to discover common ground on some basis for agreement in theology and doctrine," the assumption being "that if the parties can first reach some form of agreement about what they believe, they can turn to the more difficult issues."[13] Covenant must be a starting point in the effort to reclaim the ecumenical vision-and-vocation of our conciliar fellowship. Covenant holds significance in both UCC polity and the establishment of an ecumenical agenda in the origins of the church. Therefore, attention needs to be given to the degree to which the local congregation has been faithful to or failed in its covenantal obligations. The question then becomes how the UCC might effectively move forward in the effort to renew the covenantal agreement while reclaiming the ecumenical vision-and-vocation. I begin with a survey of the role this concept has played throughout the history of Reformed theology; within the limitations of so short a book, I can offer no more than a sketch.

The concept of covenant has a long history dating back to biblical times and beyond, while—at least in Reformed circles—the concept has often been associated with a particular theological configuration (that is, "federal theology").[14] My primary interest is in the role the term had and continues to have in the UCC as a conciliar fellowship with strong ties to the Reformed tradition. Even a cursory reading of the Reformation period discloses the utilization of the term among a number of Reformed thinkers including John Calvin, Ulrich Zwingli, and Johann H. Bullinger. The theological concept of covenant influenced both English Puritanism and theology in the New World. In general, any theological system based on the conception of covenant offered absolute assurance of God's eternal love, grace, and mercy.[15]

William Klempa affirms both "negative" and the "positive" aspects of covenant theology. He uses "covenant theology" in the formal sense of a particular methodology; even so, his assertions are relevant for my purposes. He describes the "positive" aspects as: (1) its having grounded

---

13. Stroup, "Reformed Identity," 269.

14. For a brief but helpful description of federal theology, see Klempa, "Concept of the Covenant," 100–3.

15. *Dictionary of the Presbyterian and Reformed Tradition in America*, s.v. "covenant theology."

itself in Scripture, allowing the "generative ideas or horizons of thought that enable the unity within diversity of biblical witnesses to the one God to come to expression"; (2) its success in bringing "Reformed theology down from the heights of metaphysical speculation to a living connection with history, the history of salvation"; (3) its representation of a "move in the direction of a more inclusive and universal understanding of God's work of salvation"; and (4) its ability to "hold together the sovereignty of God and human responsibility, the rightful claims of God and human freedom."[16] Associations between the four positive aspects and my previous reflections on the characteristics of ecumenicity include ideas such as "unity within diversity" and "inclusive and universal."

Comprehended in the fullness of its theological significance, covenant is filled with symbolic and ethical implications. There are difficulties with Karl Barth's explication and use of the term; still I find that his application comes closest to my intended use.[17] Arthur Cochrane argues that Barth's use of covenant is best understood, as with Barth's theology in general, as christologically informed. For Barth, humanity is assumed by the covenant of reconciliation, having been elected in Christ; a consequence of reconciliation in Christ is the election of and covenant with the *one* community of faith in *two* forms (that is, Israel and the church).[18] Barth stresses the cross of Christ as the matrix of God's completed work of redemption, which is apprehended *by* faith yet never dependent *upon* faith. Cochrane summarizes his description of Barth's use of covenant:

> The breaking down of the wall of hostility between Jews and Gentiles in the cross of Christ is the paradigm of the overcoming of all sorts of alienation and hostility between men and women, young and old, races and nations (cf. Gal. 3:28). The church is called to proclaim reconciliation as the fulfillment of the covenant in Christ in the teeth of all empirical evidence to the contrary. It is to address its message to concrete situations of alienation and hostility. Yet reconciliation as the fulfillment of the covenant is exclusively the work of God in Jesus Christ and the Holy Spirit. Humanity's work consists in the obedience of faith.[19]

16. Klempa, "Concept of the Covenant," 105–6.

17. Arthur C. Cochrane provides a short but valuable and critically constructive analysis of Barth's use of "covenant." Cochrane, "Barth's Doctrine of the Covenant," *Major Themes in the Reformed Tradition*, 108–116.

18. Ibid., 109.

19. Ibid., 111, 115.

The reference to "the obedience of faith" as personal and communal commitment implicit in this covenanted relationship is sharpened by a deeper ontological distinctive implicit in the covenantal nature of our church. My contention is based on the insights of P. Mark Achtemeier's analysis of a recently proposed document in the Presbyterian Church (USA).[20] Achtemeier states that the New Testament concept of "union with Christ" (Phil 2:1; Col 3:3; 1 Cor 1:30; 2 Tim 1:9) is picked up and emphasized repeatedly in the writings of the Protestant reformers: "Consider Calvin's understanding of the union: 'Christ, having been made ours, makes us sharers with him in the gifts with which he has been endowed' (3.11.10)."[21] Among the several benefits of this spiritual engrafting (John 15) "the believer also receives *life in Christ*, growth into the divine image."[22] Achtemeier focuses on the significance of this doctrine (*unio cum Christo*) for the unity of the church and for the "ecumenical prospects" as well.[23] The union of believers *with* Christ and the life of the church *in* Christ provide an understanding of the rudimentary nature of congregational life and mission:

> The key insight here is that participation in the trinitarian *life* of God—which is the church's communion with the Father by her union with the Son in the power of the Spirit—involves also and at the same time participation in the *mission* of God to the world. The church's union with Christ's person makes it a participant in Christ's mission, which mission is constituted by the Father's sending of the Son into the world in the power of the Spirit.[24]

20. Achtemeier, "*Union with Christ* Doctrine," 336–45.
21. Ibid., 339.
22. Ibid., 340.
23. Ibid., 345–52.
24. Ibid., 342. In the expressed ecumenical position of the UCC, the following affirmation can be found: "The goal is the *union* of the church and the *union* of creation, and mission and unity are the processes to be followed in reaching the goal." Gunnemann, *United and Uniting*, 190. It is also interesting to hear Achtemeier use the language of the "*mission* of God" as such is also used widely throughout the ecumenical literature (i.e., *missio Dei*). Darrell Guder writes: "Mission as *missio Dei* necessarily relativizes Western understandings and practices of mission. God cannot be restricted to what has been happening in Western Christianity. God's work is universal in its intention and impact, and our task is to grapple theologically with that universality. Further, it must be affirmed with the World Council of Churches that there is an 'inextricable relationship between Christian unity and missionary calling, between ecumenism and evangelization. Evangelization is the test of our ecumenical vocation.' " Guder, *Continuing Conversion of the Church*, 20, 26.

COVENANT IN ECCLESIOLOGICAL PERSPECTIVE

Covenant is central to a shared existence and common purpose in the UCC. An essential element of our self-understanding as a community of faith is the historical fact that our bond of ecclesiastical unity was forged in the early fires of ecumenicity. As an ecumenical body, we provide a "place" for a diversity of biblical and theological expressions of the one Christian faith, all within the boundaries of the unity shared and celebrated in our covenantal relationship. The covenanted nature of our unity is expressed in the language of the third article of the constitution of the church (edited for brevity and italicized for emphasis): "Within the United Church of Christ, the various expressions of the church relate to each other in a *covenantal* manner. . . . As members of the Body of Christ, each expression of the church is called to honor and respect the work and ministry of each other part. . . . In this *covenant*, the various expressions of the United Church of Christ seek to walk together in all God's ways."[25]

Louis Gunnemann recommends that the constitution of the UCC be understood as it was intended by the framers, "as the covenant that binds us in one body";[26] he argues for an ecclesiology based on the constitution as covenant. He begins discussion with a study of the preamble:[27] each of the three paragraphs constituting the preamble discloses elements essential to comprehending the constitution as covenant. Gunnemann comments on and commends each of the three as follows:

> The first paragraph makes it clear that the Constitution is the means of expressing "more fully (our) oneness in Christ." Unity given in Christ . . . is the reason for the existence of this faith community as a united and uniting church. . . . The second paragraph of the Preamble is devoted to the principle of *order*, which identifies the UCC as a body belonging to the church universal [and] Christ is the "sole Head" of the church . . . the covenant is assumed, identified primarily in the confession of Christ's headship. The UCC sees itself, therefore, as a faith community called into being by Christ, [a call that] lays claims and obligations on all who make the confession, calling them to be "kindred in Christ [with] all who share that confession." The third paragraph . . . draws out the principles of *polity* that are implicit in the *order* derived from the basic covenant . . . all members of the body—

---

25. *Constitution of the United Church of Christ*, article 3.
26. Gunnemann, *United and Uniting*, 160.
27. Ibid., 155–79.

individually and in groups—are engaged in a covenant of mutual responsibility and accountability.[28]

The local church, acknowledged to be an "autonomous" body, is also responsible for the welfare of this covenanted relationship in Christ.[29] The church is not merely a voluntary association divorced from accountability to any other body of believers; nor is the church to be regarded a loosely constituted association of like-minded people.

Such misconceptions are often found in the perceptions of many local church members, used to legitimate one's attachment to and promotion of some issue of self-interest. Paragraph 10 of the constitution "links the local church to the larger body of persons of other local churches known as the United Church of Christ." This same connectedness extends to the Church catholic as well; the congregation can be said to "exist as a United Church of Christ" to the degree that the local church acknowledges "a covenantal link with the larger communion."[30]

The ecumenical implications of this covenantal model have not been satisfactorily explored at the local level. We need to cultivate awareness of our covenantal obligations and the implications of our union *in and with* Christ. The covenanted life "involves relationships grounded in Divine forgiveness and reconciliation" as the same communion affirmed by Achtemeier: "The union of believers *with* Christ entails the union of believers with one another *in* Christ."[31] The goal is to help members of the local church better understand and appreciate the covenanted life, so that: "The coercive consequences of majority rule are intentionally countered and ameliorated for the sake of the community's unity and the individual's well-being. Learning covenant life moves beyond the democratic model of human organization to the ministerial (servant)

---

28. Ibid., 160–62.

29. Donald D. Freeman offers an incisive definition of autonomy within the framework of a covenantal relationship: "Autonomy is fundamentally *freedom for*, not merely *freedom from*. It is the highest level of personal responsibility, not irresponsibility . . . it entails a kind of freedom from the rule of others, but this is not a freedom to ignore what others command or have to say; it is freedom to listen, evaluate, decide, and act for our self through the highest exercise of rationality. Autonomy as responsibility . . . is a distinctive feature of a covenantal polity such as that of the United Church of Christ." Freeman, "Autonomy in a Covenant Polity," 2–6.

30. Gunneman, *United and Uniting*, 165.

31. Achtemeier, "*Union with Christ* Doctrine," 344.

model of life in *koinonia*. Ideally, the local church is the nurturing community for that covenantal style of life."[32]

The "covenantal style of life" commended by Gunnemann is shaped by two essential elements in every covenant: (1) a primary narrative, or story that serves as foundational to both the identity of the participants and as the historical record of ambivalence and renewal, and (2) commitment to the covenant, which shapes both the character and self-understanding of participants. The concept of covenant being promoted here is based on the biblical-theological model in which are found the key components of story and stipulation. The stipulations are grounded in the story informing the identity of both individual and community.

COVENANT AS STORY AND STIPULATION

The story itself is validated in the lived experiences of faithfulness to covenant stipulations that must be fulfilled by individual and community. A union of story and stipulation provides a full-bodied comprehension of the term *covenant*,[33] depicting characteristics of God's involvement with the community of faith and shaping the nature of the covenantal relationship shared by members of that same community:

> Participational decision-making as exercised on behalf of self-serving concerns is displaced in the churches even in the wider society. The only corrective to the misuse of participational decision-making lies in the recognition that in the church responsible relationships among the people are under the discipline of the lordship of Christ. The church's distinctive characteristic is concern that the form of the church may demonstrate a new community rooted in a new covenant mediated between God and God's people through Jesus Christ.[34]

---

32. Gunnemann, *United and Uniting*, 169.

33. "The covenant God made with us, with Israel, with the world, is a command premised relationship. The covenant is based in command, and God expects to be obeyed. There are, moreover, sanctions and consequences of disobedience that cannot be avoided, even as there are gifts and joys along with obedience. The Torah is given for guidance, so that Israel (and all Israel's belated heirs) are "clued in" to the defining expectations of this relationship in an Agent with will and purpose that must be taken seriously and cannot be disregarded or mocked." Brueggemann, *Covenanted Self*, 17.

34. Gunnemann, *Shaping of the United Church of Christ*, 200. A helpful discussion of the same issue can also be found in Paul, *Freedom with Order*, 76–81.

Stephen Crites draws a distinction between mundane and sacred stories. The former are those accounts which replicate our everyday experiences in narrative form, while the latter have a more transcendent quality, taking on a life of their own. Though distinct, the two forms are related so that "between sacred and mundane stories there is a distinction without separation . . . mundane stories are implicit in [the] sacred story, and every mundane story takes its soundings in the sacred story. But some mundane stories sound out greater depths than others . . . myths and epics, even scriptures, are mundane stories. But in these . . . the sacred stories resonate. People are able to feel this resonance, because the unalterable stories are those they know best of all."[35]

Sections of the preamble to the constitution include both mundane and sacred narratives. The narrative implicit in the reference to the biblical account of salvation and the "faith of the historic church" represents the sacred story, while the reference to the historical realities of our antecedent and catholic ancestry as a church represents the mundane. Mundane and sacred stories are distinct yet without separation; the nature of the relationship between these two narrative forms is such that together they shape identity. We too, as a covenanted community of faith, are bound together by virtue of our sharing these stories, with all of their implied diversity and ambiguity; it is the relatedness of sacred and mundane stories that discloses the dynamic meaning of the covenant we share.

COVENANT IN BIBLICAL PERSPECTIVE

In the biblical story, we witness the covenanted intentions of God; the sacred story of redemption and the mundane story of God's people dramatize the covenant as having been established, violated, reconciled, and renewed. Initiated by God, the covenant has two inseparable parts: "Grace does not will only to be received and known. It wills also to rule. There is no grace without the lordship and claim of grace."[36] Accordingly, the doctrine of God's gracious election is followed by the doctrine of God's commandment as God's "claim, decision, and judgment upon humanity."[37] The covenant represents a history of communion in which sacred and mundane stories, command and commitment, story and stipulation are inseparable.

35. Crites, "Narrative Quality of Experience," 70.
36. Cochrane, "Barth's Doctrine of the Covenant," 108.
37. Ibid., 114.

A biblical paradigm for my position on covenant is found in the Book of Deuteronomy. Remembrance and recitation of the normative stories of redemption are Israel's means of reinforcing identity and shared faith convictions as a covenanted community. In Deuteronomy, remembering is more than a cognitive act; it means living in a particular way, a way of life that is in accord with the storied stipulations of the covenant. One of the more intriguing characteristics of Deuteronomy is the authorization it provides for a faithful reinterpretation of both story and stipulations.[38] Stated in more exact terms:

> Just as Deuteronomy reinterpreted old traditions in the light of more current situations, so we are authorized to reinterpret both scripture and tradition in our own time. Yet this is always done under the critical eye of both the whole counsel/council of God, and the ever present community of believers. As members of a covenanted-community we honor both scripture and tradition as more than an historical account open to manipulation and distortion.[39]

Deuteronomy combines the joy of God's story with the free and faithful response of the people to God's stipulations, which models what it means to live as a covenanted community. God's people are shaped and identified by the redemptive narrative of a loving Lord; the specifics of the stipulations commanded, as an expression of God's grace, elicit a free and joyful fulfillment of covenanted obligations fostering peace, harmony, and unity.

Likewise, the covenanted relationship of our conciliar fellowship cannot be relegated to the ranks of mere human fabrication or convenience, intended to force the opinions and theological convictions of some on the greater whole. The covenant shared among churches of the UCC bears an ontological implication of no lesser significance than that which is evident in the sacrament of baptism in which there is identifica-

---

38. See the second paragraph to the preamble: "[The UCC] claims as its own the faith of the historic Church expressed in the ancient creeds and reclaimed in the basic insights of the Protestant Reformers. It affirms the responsibility of the Church in each generation to make this faith its own in reality of worship, in honesty of thought and expression, and in purity of heart before God." *Constitution of the United Church of Christ*, 2.

39. Throughout this portion dealing with the Book of Deuteronomy as paradigmatic I am indebted to the insights of Patrick Miller (unpublished lecture presented at Princeton Theological Seminary).

tion between us and Christ.⁴⁰ Not only the quality but the very subject of our lives is transformed by entrance into this covenanted community. Violating this covenantal relationship creates a wound in the body of Christ, as separation alters the being of those who choose some lesser standard of communal existence.

Both freedom and faithfulness are more than possibilities; they are in fact actualities in Christ who stands at the *center* of the covenant shared. Jesus' prayer in the gospel of John must be read in the context of his commandment that his followers love one another. "Jesus' prayer discloses both the mystery of grace by which alone the commandment can be kept and the communal context of shared life to which Jesus prayer concretely refers."⁴¹

Responding to Christ's expressed desire for unity and advancing that desire at the local level necessitates a proper understanding of the covenantal relationship and the ecumenical vision-and-vocation that have been essential to the UCC from its inception. Members of the local church need to be encouraged to reclaim and rejuvenate the vision-and-vocation with which their church was given birth:

> The United Church of Christ was born within time of ferment generated by the mandate of Christian unity and the consequent denominational self-examination. In the midst of that ferment the Congregational Christian Churches and the Evangelical and Reformed Church *rediscovered their kinship.* Drawn together in a time of great human need for the healing that only the gospel can offer, a shared religious orientation, and a common theological tradition, these two communions were able to transcend the differences their individual histories had produced to experience a renewal.⁴²

---

40. Paragraph B9 of the document *Baptism, Eucharist, and Ministry* states that: "Baptism is related not only to momentary experience, but to a life-long growth into Christ. Those baptized are called upon to reflect the glory of the Lord as they are transformed by the power of the Holy Spirit, into his likeness, with ever increasing splendor (II Cor.3:18). The life of the Christian is necessarily one of continuing struggle yet also of continuing experience of grace. In this new relationship, the baptized live for the sake of Christ, of his Church and of the world which he loves, while they wait in hope for the manifestation of God's new creation and for the time when God will be all in all (Rom. 8:18–24; I Cor. 15:22–28, 49–57)." World Council of Churches, *Faith and Order, Baptism, Eucharist, and Ministry: Faith and Order Paper No.111*, http//www.wcc-coc.org/wcc/what/faith/bem.2.html.

41. Braaten and Jenson, *In One Body*, 32.

42. Gunnemann, *Shaping of the United Church of Christ*, 135.

One should not underestimate the level of both courage and humility necessary on behalf of those who first fostered and then sought to fulfill the vision of a Christian body dedicated to the pursuit of unity among fellow believers; of equal importance, one cannot underestimate the courage and humility it will require of those who now seek to pursue that same vision-and-vocation even further and do so with the firm conviction that it is done in obedience to the command and prayerful petition of the Lord Christ. The concept of covenant will continue to play a key role in this process because it symbolizes the willingness to move well beyond the boundaries of one's own cherished traditions, with genuine openness and humility of heart, and to do more than merely acknowledge the credibility of traditions other than one's own. It will necessitate the courage to enter into covenant with those whose traditions, ways of worship, and habits of devotion are foreign, and to embrace them favorably as manifestations of the one grace of the triune God given to a community of faith different from one's own. We know that in the kingdom of God those differences we now cherish will melt away and the commonality of our fellowship in Christ will be all that remains; our ecumenical mission is to replicate that same truth now, here, and by the grace of God in the power of the Holy Spirit.

8

Place as Metaphor: Theological and Biblical Basis

PLACE CAN BE PERCEIVED metaphorically, with deep currents of symbolic meaning. Having *place* represents the environment of well-being and the nurture of one's sense of self (identity formation). In the generic sense of the term, place can also represent security, community, rootedness, connectedness, etc. The metaphoric value of place is in its representation of the covenantal relationship in which one is placed, at home. In this sense, place is where conciliar identity is validated and nurtured; it is the environment wherein one's ecumenicity can be expressed freely and can be in union with others of a "like mind."[1] Shifting the metaphoric focus, place represents what George Stroup (following Ludwig Wittgenstein) refers to as a "family resemblance" in which "there is a discernable similarity between grammars of faith and the forms of life that accompany them."[2]

The term *place* has also played a role in the language of the wider ecumenical movement where the word is often used in reference to a specific geographic and cultural locale of the church yet suggests a metaphoric

---

1. My use of "like mind" is a modification of what George W. Stroup, in his analysis of the writing of Brian Gerrish, calls "habitas." Gerrish argues that there are five characteristics of the Reformed concept of "habitas" (or "habit of mind"): "it is, first, 'deferential (that is, it respects tradition); second, the Reformed habit is critical (especially of the tradition it reveres); third, it is open to wisdom wherever it can be found; fourth, the Reformed habit of mind is unabashedly practical (truth is in order to goodness); and, fifth, the foremost note is the evangelical habit (the overwhelming prophetic sense of standing, as Jeremiah was, under the Word of the Lord that we dare not tamper with and which does not let us remain silent)." Stroup states that *"habitas* is characterized by simplicity, and according to the Heidelberg Catechism, by thanksgiving or gratitude, not simply gratitude as something that is believed, but also as something that is lived." Stroup, "Reformed Identity," 263–64.

2. Ibid., 264.

meaning as well.³ In an address presented to a consultation of the World Council of Churches on the meaning of the term "local church," Lesslie Newbigin made use of the word *place* in a fashion I intend as well:

> The relation of the Church to the *place* is to be understood christologically; the relation of the Church to its *place* is to be governed by the relation of Christ to the world. That relation may be described in a threefold way. Christ is the Word through whom all things were made and in whom they have their being; therefore the Church in each place, being itself part of the secular reality of that place, is to love and cherish all of it in its created goodness. Christ is the one in whom all things are to be consummated and to find their true reconciliation; therefore the Church in each place is to be a sign of the true end for which everything in the secular reality of that place exists. Christ is the one who has been made flesh, died and risen again in order to take away the sins of the world and to reconcile all to the Father; therefore the Church in each place, always "bearing about the body of the dying Jesus," sharing through him in the messianic tribulations which are the mark of the continuing conflict between the reign of God and the power of evil, will also manifest in its life the victorious life of the risen Jesus (II Cor. 4:10).⁴

Thus the church in each place is to be the sign, planted in the midst of the present realities of the place but pointing beyond them to the future that God has promised; an instrument available for God's use in the doing of God's will for that place; a foretaste—manifesting and enjoying already in the midst of the messianic tribulation, a genuine foretaste of the peace and joy of God's reign. As often as it gathers to hear God's

---

3. The words of Hugo Rahner, as found in an article written in 1963 as one in a collection of articles on the nature of the church, continue to have painful relevance to the contemporary setting in which the church seeks to serve the world with the Word of grace and in the power of the Holy Spirit. Rahner wrote: "Look about in this world—everywhere there is desert, aimless wandering, thirst that cannot be quenched, strangers who no longer know home. But in this desert you see a thornbush burst into flames, and you hear the divine words: 'The place where you stand is holy ground' (Exod. 3:5). This is a type, a model of the holy Church. She is a wretched, prickly shrub in the desert, but even now she bursts into flames with heavenly fire. Here we stand: we believe in this Church of weak brambles and tremendous fire. She is our trial of faith and our love's joy." Rahner, "The Church, God's Strength," 14. I would merely add that the church is also and always the only genuine respite for those longing to find peace and joy, renewal and recreation, and fulfillment of life as God has intended; it is in church that one is gifted with "place," with "home," with acceptance that is of eternal length and breadth!

4. Note the striking similarity between the theological language of Newbigin at this point and that of Körtner.

word and to share in the eucharistic celebration, that church is renewed as the body of Christ in and for that place.[5]

The Old Testament scriptures maintain a very clear connection between symbolic representation and geographic locale (for example, in the theological use of "Zion" or "Jerusalem" as the "mount and city of God," or in the use of Jerusalem's Temple). A shift in the conceptual and metaphoric use of the term place is immediately evident in the New Testament scriptures. In John 2:19-21, Jesus makes reference to his *body* in the metaphoric sense of a "temple" superior to that which stood at the heart of Jerusalem. In the letter of 1 Peter 2:4-8, reference is made to the community of faith as a "spiritual house" (2:5) of which the members are "living stones" (2:5), with the crucified and risen Christ as the "living Stone" (2:5) upon which the church has been founded. As Philip Porter has written:

> It is this image and understanding of the living house which has motivated the ecumenical movement. As is well known, the word ecumenical is derived for the Greek word *oikoumene*, meaning the whole inhabited earth. The ecumenical movement is . . . the means by which the churches which form the house, the *oikos* of God, are seeking so to live and witness before all people that the whole *oikoumene* may become the *oikos* of God through the crucified and risen Christ in the power of the life-giving Spirit.[6]

Place, as metaphor and theological referent, is derived from the rich biblical study of the use of "land" in the Old Testament by Walter Brueggemann. Brueggemann argues that throughout the Old Testament "land" is a major metaphoric and theological theme. In one of his earlier works Brueggemann states that for Israel:

> Place is space which has historical meaning [providing] continuity and identity across generations. Place is space in which important words have been spoken which have established identity, defined vocation and envisioned destiny. Place is a complex network of relationships, connections and continuities . . . of physical, social and cultural conditions that describe my actions, my responses, my awareness and that give shape and content to the very life that is me; a yearning for a place is a decision to enter history with an identifiable people in an identifiable pilgrimage.[7]

---

5. Newbigin, "What Is 'a Local Church Truly United'?" 114.
6. Porter, "Gathered for Life," 54-55.
7. Brueggemann, *The Land*, 5.

In reference to the New Testament scriptures, Philip Sheldrake claims that while the "particularity of place could not be bypassed entirely given the fundamental nature of the doctrine of the Incarnation, it is also clear" from the foundational New Testament texts "that there was a different and urgent concern for Christian disciples . . . to move out from what was local to them, from 'home,' into the entire world, the *oikoumene*."[8] This missionary thrust eventually meant that for the earliest Christians "God was increasingly to be worshiped in whatever place they found themselves . . . the experience of 'being in transit,' of journey, became the central metaphor for the encounter with and response to God. For the disciples, significant conversion experiences often occur 'on the way' in situations of . . . transition."[9]

Much of the New Testament speaks of *place* with incarnational, relational, and communal characteristics attached to its meaning (e.g., John 1:1–4; Heb 13:13; Rev 21:1–4, 22–26). Other New Testament passages testify to the theological significance of the correspondence between *place* and individual as well as corporate identity (e.g., Eph 2:19–22; 1 Cor 3:9, 16; 12:27; Col 3:1–4; Heb 10:19–21). The most commonly employed metaphor is the Pauline "body of Christ,"[10] which Anders Nygren contends refers as much to the reality of the local congregation as it does the universal church. It is through the sacrament of baptism that one is given a "place" as a member of the body of Christ:

> Through baptism the Christian has been incorporated into Christ; he [or she] is a member of the body, a branch which has been grafted into the vine and is not united with it and a part of it. In the mind of Paul a person who has been united with Christ through baptism no longer has an independent existence, but is simply and solely a member of his body. In baptism we have been incorporated into Christ's body and we are now his own members.[11]

Furthermore, the ecumenical document, *Baptism, Eucharist and Ministry*, affirms that through baptism, "Christians are brought into union with Christ, with each other and with the Church of every time

---

8. Sheldrake, *Spaces for the Sacred*, 33.

9. Ibid., 34.

10. For one of the more helpful discussions of the NT phrase "body of Christ" in an ecumenical context, see: Nygren, *Christ and His Church*, 93–100.

11. Ibid., 105.

and place. Our common baptism, which unites us to Christ in faith, is thus a basic bond of unity."[12] Our "place" is "in/with" Christ.

"PLACE" AS "HOME"

M. Craig Barnes makes use of another metaphor that adds depth and pastoral integrity to my use of the term *place*.[13] While his book is, on the whole, disassociated from the specificities of my thesis, themes and insights found in his work are applicable: for example, his central metaphor of *home*. After an introduction to the topic by use of a personal narrative, Barnes describes the contemporary culture as one in which there is a "longing for home" evident in the restlessness and searching of our contemporaries. He relates this same experience to a similar theme found throughout the Bible, as persons wander "from one disconnected experience to the next," uncertain that they will ever again know the security of having a *place* of their own.[14] Barnes defines "home" in language that resonates with my use of *place*, stating that home is "the right place, the place where we belong, where we know who we are . . . it is the place where the sacred communion has been restored and made right."[15]

Home "isn't so much a geographical place" as it is a metaphor for "the heart of God where we are created to dwell."[16] At first blush it would seem as though our purposes diverge, yet I believe that the use of theological language like "the heart of God" is not all that distant from the intent of language like being "in Christ." Barnes draws even closer to an associated use when he asserts that from its inception "the church has always thought about home more in terms of community" where "a community consists of relationships."[17] His comment reiterates ecumenical themes such as *koinonia* and *oikoumene*, terms essential to the formation of conciliar identity.

Communion in the triune life has become one of several ecclesiological foci associated with the ecumenical movement. The opening paragraph from the "Report of the Section on Unity" issued from the third assembly of the WCC in New Delhi in 1961 states that "the love of the Father and the Son in the unity of the Holy Spirit is the source

12. *Baptism, Eucharist and Ministry*, "Commentary (B6)," 6.
13. Barnes, *Searching for Home*.
14. Ibid., 17–21.
15. Ibid., 17.
16. Ibid., 33.
17. Ibid.

and goal of the unity which the Triune God wills for all [humans] and creation. We believe that we share in this unity in the Church of Jesus Christ."[18] Elaborating on the concept of our being "in Christ," Barnes avers that "we are made part of the triune family of Father, Son, and Spirit. That is our home . . . where we belong, and we will never be content with any place other than that communion."[19]

Barnes extends the concept of "home" as a metaphor for ending one's spiritual meandering with three other metaphors descriptive of the historical stages leading up to our contemporary displacement and concomitant homelessness. He speaks of the cultural transition from "shelters" to "exiles" to "nomads."[20] The postwar (WWII) ethos of building communities that resembled the "small towns" of an earlier historical period was soon followed by the "exilic" consciousness of the economic boom and prosperity era, where one's life was shaped more by the emerging lifestyle of materialism and where "exiles were stuck with jobs that they didn't really like, but had to keep in order to afford a lifestyle they didn't much like either."[21]

As the suburban exiles became less and less enamored of the lifestyle they once considered just this side of "heaven on earth," culture transitioned to the "nomadic" lifestyle, where we slide easily from place to place, from identity to identity, which is precisely why the longing for home is greater than ever. . . . We don't want another self-help book, exercise program, promotion, or even another intimate relationship. We just want to rest. But for that we need a home.[22]

As the philosophical trappings and the *pseudo*-spirituality of *post*-traditional culture begin to wane, and as the accompanying worldview no longer functions to provide meaning, local church members join others in the search for foundational beliefs and connections of a different order. This time of searching is an opportunity for members to discover the dynamic resources awaiting them in the substantive convictions and faith statements that are foundational to the UCC. Our own conciliar fellowship is established on the desire to seek unity, wholeness, communion in the church as paradigmatic of the greater unity and promised

---

18. Kinnamon, *Vision of the Ecumenical Movement*, 153.
19. Barnes, *Searching for Home*, 35.
20. Ibid., esp. 37–69.
21. Ibid., 47–48.
22. Ibid., 49–50.

Place as Metaphor: Theological and Biblical Basis   69

wholeness of all things in the kingdom of God. This identity configuration is based upon the need for wholeness as the *place* of rest (i.e., *shalom* as "Sabbath" rest). It is the movement toward the "home" with "foundations, whose architect and builder is God" (Heb 11:10).

Barnes writes: "You have to give yourself to a place before you can belong, and you have to belong before you can receive anything of eternal value from that place—things like the defining convictions for life."[23] In giving themselves to the ecumenical vision and vocation of the UCC, members of the local church discover where it is they do belong; the spiritual value in such belonging and the faith convictions of conciliar identity shape a particular Christian lifestyle with a primary focus on the ministry of reconciliation.

Barnes's proposal addresses another issue of central importance to my proposal: "The divine reality is that we are often thrown together with people we don't particularly like, and certainly don't resemble. But when that community has a common axis mundi at its center, it not only holds together but also holds heaven to earth . . . defined at the center this community doesn't worry about boundary issues and can accommodate all sorts of diversity . . . because it holds together by having clarity about the center."[24]

Notice how he uses terminology encountered in ecumenical circles, e.g., "accommodating diversity." More importantly he emphasizes the "common axis mundi" which is essential to the formation of conciliar identity as well. In more exacting terms, Barnes writes: "When we allow the story of our lives to be rooted in a story greater than ourselves, we are not limited to the small house that we can construct for ourselves."[25] That "small house" we "construct for ourselves" can look very much like the constricted space of a narrowly defined denominational or confessional identity.

Set up in isolation, ghettoized by the too restrictive walls of personal pride in a "place" of our own creation, little room remains for communion with neighbors whose differences we find threatening or unacceptable. It is more fitting to the character of conciliar identity for local church members to share the perspective of Roger Shinn when he writes that "the United Church of Christ draws its faith and life primarily from the Great

23. Ibid., 57.
24. Ibid., 60.
25. Ibid., 67.

Story." The components of the "Great Story" include the Story of God, human history, as well as human hope and expectation. While drawing its "faith and life" from the Story of God, the UCC does so

> within the context of its own lesser story, the story of a church with a short history but with roots that go far back in time. Its faith is not simply the faith of an American church, formally organized as recently as June 25, 1957. It is a faith shared with prophets and apostles throughout the ages. But it is that faith as understood in our time and place by a community of Christians who believe that we have something to contribute to, and much to learn from, the other and wider community of which we are a part.[26]

Barnes describes the church as our "home away from home" drawing upon some of those same New Testament images already considered as metaphors for the term *place*. He affirms an essential ecclesiological assertion of the wider ecumenical movement:

> The church . . . is only the Body of Christ to the degree that it finds its life, mission, and hope in Christ. There is no other basis for this household to exist, no other means by which it will serve the world around it as a sanctifying and redemptive presence, and no other hope for it to be the tabernacle leading us home. None of that is possible apart from being a community "in" Christ.[27]

Even though his use of theological terminology differs from my own (for example, where he would use "dissettlement" and "nomadic existence," I prefer "displacement"), Barnes's aim is to encourage the experience of genuine community that is of necessity dependent upon a true sense of belonging. He states as a generality an experience I have addressed in concrete situations and real lives of local church members who, "after swallowing too many introspective therapies and self awareness books, [become] convinced that when they look deep within themselves they find nothing. . . . Even an empty soul knows it was created for something more."[28]

As a pastoral concern, this raises the question: how could this be the case when these same "souls" are connected to an ecumenical vision-and-vocation as rich as that which sustains the UCC? Stated as

---

26. Shinn, *Confessing Our Faith*, 3–4.
27. Barnes, *Searching for Home*, 147.
28. Ibid., 178.

a challenge: perhaps the fact that there are far too many members of the local church struggling with this void of spiritual meaning indicates that the richness of the church's ecumenical vision-and-vocation has not impacted their lives to any significant degree, if it has at all. I offer one model in which ecumenicity is understood to have far greater promise than another prepackaged program for church membership development and denominational identity formation. Adapting the words of Barnes for my purpose:

> Implicit in the [ecumenical] recognition of faith, beyond our denominational identities, is the [conciliar] affirmation, that other churches have a legitimate means of grace, a proclamation that the sacrifice of Jesus is heaven's way for us to come home, and in Christ we can experience Triune communion today.[29]

---

29. Ibid., 179.

9

Some Critical Observations

ULRICH KÖRTNER ARGUES THAT "the ecumenical idea has expanded from a movement within the churches to a *Weltanschauung*, a view of the world, which makes the idea of unity the guiding principle for the future of humankind as such."[1] Embracing the veracity of his observation, my project maintains a modest goal, providing pastors and lay people with a viable option.

The larger issue is this: the unity of the church is said to represent a promise to the whole of creation; the vision-and-vocation of the UCC cannot be confined to the unity of the church only, but must press on and, under the guidance of the Holy Spirit, seek the reconciliation of all things in Christ (see 2 Cor 5:18–21). In these efforts, we must acknowledge that "the varieties of ecumenism do not easily harmonize with one another."[2] Concentration on the local congregation as the axis for the development of conciliar identity does not imply a disinterest in the social and justice issues of the world. The local church is that "place" or "home" in which the member discovers his or her identity as a "conciliar" disciple enlarged and engaged in ecumenical ministries at the local level, but to such an extent that they will impact the real needs of the larger world as well.[3]

---

1. Körtner, "Paradox Catholicity," 399.
2. Ibid.
3. "The needs of this threatened and divided world are universal in scope, and they are supremely matched by the gospel, itself universal in scope. It is not fitting for the Reformed family—or any other Christian family—so to partition reality that Christians can proclaim only a local message and perhaps find it difficult or even impossible to communicate with their remoter brothers and sisters.

"Those who have by grace been grasped by the vision of evangelical catholicity that is integral to the Reformed tradition, those who really believe in being reformed by the Spirit through the Word discerned within the fellowship—such have no alternative but

Some Critical Observations 73

The UCC assumed the features of a "denomination" almost from the start,[4] perhaps as the inevitable consequence of the institutionalization of the church. Even though this newly formed church body, in the midst of developing a viable organizational structure, continued to pursue the founding ecumenical vision,[5] such efforts had a marginal effect at the level of the local church. The vision with which this church began as a "movement," had not lost its "verve,"[6] but it failed to find ownership among members of the local church, who remained, for the most part, inadequately informed. Therefore local church membership has not been equipped to carry out its important role in the propagation of that same vision-and-vocation for the sake of the church and world, re-

---

to affirm their gospel and to live by it in all spheres: ecclesiastical, intellectual, sociopolitical. Nor is it simply a matter of getting our theory straight as individuals or living consistently as individuals. It is a matter of fellowship." Sell, *Reformed, Evangelical, Catholic Theology*, 235–36.

4. Louis Gunnemann makes two pertinent comments. He states that in the formation of the United Church of Christ, the hope to overcome the "evils of denominationalism" was "expressed in a variety of ways by the architects of the union, who, in their Evangelical and Reformed or Congregational Christian experience, had either intuitively or rationally concluded the need to address the changing situation of American church life. Such idealistic motives should not be discounted, even though a study of the development of the new denomination shows a complex of forces working toward union." And yet in the formation of that new denomination "whatever particular characteristics it may retain from its European heritage have been transmuted within the religious atmosphere that elevates freedom of choice and freedom of dissent above all authoritarian dictums. Moreover, the occasion of its birth at a point in American religious history that is receiving special attention—the Fifties and Sixties—is of critical significance in understanding the dilemmas of denominationalism, which are reflected repeatedly in its development." Gunneman, *Shaping of the United Church of Christ*, 18, 19.

5. "In view of ever-widening opportunities for further explicit moves toward church union," the Commission on Christian Unity and Ecumenical Study and Service "sought from the Fourth General Synod in 1963 a definitive statement about union. That statement, adopted by the General Synod, affirmed: 'We believe that the Head of the church calls us to reunion, to renewal, and to the world. In the faith that God speaks a relevant and saving Word to the faithful, *the United Church of Christ is ready to lose its life, if need be*, that Christ's Church may become visibly one.' " Ibid., 83. I can only surmise that there would be few lay people in the churches in which I have served as a pastor who would deny the same affirmation as an expression of their confessional commitment; I can also hope that with the advance of conciliar identity that same affirmation could be more naturally assumed as an expression of one's own faith conviction.

6. Guder argues that "the real problem . . . is not that movements become institutions. The problem is what happens to the central and driving mission of the movement when this transition takes place. Bosch speaks of this problem as a 'loss of much of [the movement's] verve.' " Guder, *Continuing Conversion of the Church*, 187–88.

signing furtherance of both to denominational officers and ministries of the national church. We need to recall that "according to the Reformed understanding, the congregation is not the smallest cell of a church that exists above it. It does not represent a church existing apart from it but is viewed as the nucleus of a church that develops out of it. This decentralized, congregation-oriented ecclesiology is mobile enough to enter into the highly different living conditions of churches with different challenges. The Reformed tradition is, in line with its essence, an ecumenical tradition directed at plurality and difference."[7]

I am not encouraging reclamation of the past as a means to redeem a loss of tradition. I do not wish to promote a memory of "better days" before the UCC became mired in the swamps of social action and political agendas, perceived by myself and others to be responsible for the decline of doctrinal standards and the hemorrhaging of members and the dissolving of ties by local congregations. Nor am I arguing that the church, local or wider, *must* regain a clear self-awareness or a firm identity as a means to resolve all current issues and problems with even more divisive results. I agree with Michael Weinrich when he assesses the implicit danger in discussing the importance of "identity," in particular when identity is thought to be a panacea for the multiplicity of the church's current problems. Weinrich contends that

> the concept of identity seems to have brought with it precisely that which the church has not infrequently attacked as the modern "mania of finding oneself." In this use the extremely blurry concept of identity acquires the profile that one becomes aware of oneself and through the description of one's distinction from others is invigorated in order thus to strengthen one's own self-awareness . . . the problem arises not only from the fact that the church wishes to be something for itself but also and primarily from the fact that it believes it can recapture this on the basis of the strengths of its particular tradition.[8]

Weinrich's critical comment has been confirmed as the reality in almost every case where local churches have chosen to separate from the local conference and the UCC; the congregation has voted to reclaim either the title "Evangelical and Reformed," "Covenant," or "Christ's Church," and sometimes simply "Reformed." Here "identity" is misused,

---

7. Weinrich, "Openness and Worldliness of the Church," 416–17.
8. Ibid., 431.

a product of sincere but misguided and theologically muddled thinking, which deepens divisions in the body and adds to the number of "separated" brethren.[9]

Conciliar identity advances the respectful acceptance of difference and the desire to pursue visible signs of unity. Again, and in the words of Weinrich:

> To be church does not consist simply in being a church, and therefore the preservation of tradition and identity cannot be its decisive perspectives for reform. Rather, it belongs to its confessional existence to confess continually more than it is and than it can ever present. It is not to itself that it has to witness in the "world" but to the reconciliation and the coming of the Kingdom of God in word and deed. If the church can find its way to its "confessional" existence in this sense, it could also turn again decisively to its special mission.[10]

GENUINE CATHOLICITY

I do not use "catholicity," and the openness implied in that title, to legitimate all actions of inclusivity in the UCC; nor do I advocate the use of openness, as the catholic nature of the church, to condone all actions the UCC has taken in the name of "tolerance." There can be no genuine inclusivity without an appropriate and, at times, necessary exclusivity. Ecumenicity demands both critical and constructive engagements (admonitions as well as affirmations), or the claim of a *catholic* unity will

---

9. While the use of "separated brethren" is borrowed from the language of Vatican II, it is not intended to suggest that Protestant communions are to be understood as belonging, at a deeper level, to the "one true (Roman Catholic) church," but implies that while divisions exist and we are "separated" in form, we are united (in Christ) in our essential nature as "brethren." See Lambert, *Ecumenism*, 498–99, 506–7, 510. I do wish, however, that the churches that have chosen to sever their covenantal ties with the UCC would heed the reasonable advice of Bernard Lambert: "In a dialogue, no good results from bitter criticism of one's own Church or denomination. Whatever its defects or deficiencies may be, whatever its spiritual wealth or poverty, it has been responsible for the upbringing of each of us, and if a man [or woman] has been born into a denomination, even if it is the oddest denomination, it has been the means of his [her] becoming a Christian. To shirk this fact through embarrassment or to pretend that it does not exist, is of no avail, and such criticism foisted on another in order to display 'broad-mindedness' does fundamentally harm mutual esteem. Defects have to be admitted, of course, but the way this is done makes all the difference." Ibid., 501.

10. Ibid., 433.

ring hollow. The church has never embraced all persons or all beliefs in some form of blind inclusiveness; she has been firm in her "yes" but equally firm in her "no"! Conciliar identity treats catholicity with the same depth and breadth of wisdom evident in the definition of *catholic* as found in the writing of Vincent of Lerins when he counsels that "every care should be taken to hold fast to what has been believed everywhere, always, and by all."[11]

THEORETICAL FOUNDATIONS

The argument of this book has not been generated in a vacuum; I am committed to that expression of the catholic faith that is "Reformed" in nature. What I honor most in that same tradition is the ecumenical characteristic that has been evident throughout the long history of this confessional community's existence. It is from within the richness of this same tradition that I seek to address the issue of identity formation.

George Stroup has described "Reformed identity" by reference to several categories: "polity," "essential tenets," "themes and emphases," "habitas," and the "cultural-linguistic model."[12] Two of the five play a central role in the theoretical foundation of my proposal (i.e., "habitas" and "cultural-linguistic"). "Habitas" is derived from the work of Brian Gerrish and the term "cultural-linguistic" is derived from the writing of George Lindbeck.[13] "Habitas" has been defined by Gerrish as the cultivation of "good habits of mind, all of which rest fully on the one foundation which is Jesus Christ."[14] The term "cultural-linguistic" is based on language taken primarily from George Lindbeck's groundbreaking study in Christian doctrine.[15]

---

11. Lerins, "Commonitories," 270. Elaborating on the abbreviated "everywhere, always, and by all," Vincent of Lerins states that the truly "Catholic" comprises everything universal and as a "general rule" the church should always follow the principles of "universality, antiquity, and consent . . . in regard to universality if we confess that faith alone to be true which the entire Church confesses all over the world . . . in regard to antiquity if we in no way deviate from those interpretations which our ancestors . . . have manifestly proclaimed as inviolable . . . in regard to consent, if, in the very antiquity, we adopt the definitions and propositions of all, or almost all, the bishops and doctors." Ibid., 270–71.

12. Stroup, "Reformed Identity," 259–65.

13. For an extended discussion of the contribution and value of Lindbeck's proposal to the present work, I refer the reader to chapter 10 of this book.

14. Ibid., 263.

15. Lindbeck, *Nature of Doctrine*.

Some Critical Observations 77

According to Stroup, Lindbeck's work is based in part on the thought of Ludwig Wittgenstein, who spoke of "family resemblances" and the "form of life" given shape by the particularities of specific linguistic configurations in any given culture or community. Stroup states that "family resemblances" form "a helpful and attractive metaphor that can be used to describe identity in the midst of diversity."[16] The cultural-linguistic model, while useful in the discussion of identity, is dependent on the insights of cultural anthropology and limited in providing theological categories. Stroup contends that this model also neglects the importance of history in the formation of communities and their respective languages. Nevertheless, he values the model as one "tool" among others available to the theologian as a premise for understanding the complexities of identity formation.[17]

Taking up the issue of "family resemblance," and more particularly in terms of a shared language or grammar, Stroup focuses on the use of confessions in the Reformed tradition. Throughout history Reformed confessions have been judged as interpretations of the gospel, summarizations of doctrine for use in worship and education in faith. They have also been used to express the deep convictions of the Christian community, often addressed to some critical issue in the life of the church. In concluding his argument, Stroup writes:

Although the Reformed confessions use different language to express (faith) convictions, they share a common grammar, and as a whole they constitute a kind of "textbook" by which one learns to speak, feel, and understand the Reformed faith. In this sense the Reformed confessions are not so much a series of tenets one must believe as they are a language, a grammar, and a way of speaking, feeling, and living. It may be that the grammar of the Reformed confessions not only enables one to name religious and theological realities in one's experience, but the language and grammar may themselves create or at least mediate that experience.[18]

Examining the *UCC Statement of Faith*, Roger Shinn affirms that the antecedent traditions of the UCC "had rich inheritances of confessional documents" including "the ancient creeds imbedded in scripture and developed in the early centuries of the church."[19] The decision to draft a "statement" rather than a "creed" was driven by a "more modest

16. Stroup, "Reformed Identity," 264.
17. Ibid., 265–68.
18. Ibid., 267.
19. Shinn, *Confessing Our Faith*, 5.

attempt to say what it is that contemporary Christians believe."[20] The statement of faith has no legal status, in the sense that its use is required; it is "an effort to find a language appropriate for Christian testimony. But the statement of faith, as a testimony of Christian conviction, is adding to life no test that is not inherent in Christian existence."[21]

Shinn advises that any statement of faith must honor the creedal tradition of the Church catholic, maintaining the relationship between the faith confessed and the life lived, that is, between belief and practice. The union of belief and practice is achieved in the *UCC Statement of Faith*.[22] The second point Shinn makes, even more decisive for my purpose, is his contention that the statement of faith has an "ecumenical purpose"; it does not intend to "state the peculiar faith of the people who came together in the United Church of Christ; it aims to state the Christian faith as this church, in conversation with other groups of Christians, apprehends that faith."[23] Shinn illuminates that portion of the statement which gives testimony to the reality of the church; his comments clarify the most basic elements of an ecclesiology representative of the UCC. He develops his commentary by way of four convictions implicit in the wording.

The first conviction affirms, "It is God, the Holy Spirit, who creates the church. This church is not a creation of and not a possession of men and women . . . when the churches defy God they falsify their nature and calling." The second asserts, "The Holy Spirit ceaselessly works for the renewal of the church. The church is always under judgment, always in need of renewal . . . *ecclesia reformata, semper reformanda*. God's church, in a distinctive way, lives under the mandate for renewal and acknowledges the renewing power of the Holy Spirit." In the third conviction, "The church is a covenant people . . . the Christian covenant is not simply an agreement between consenting people, who are free to break it by mutual agreement. It's a covenant between people of faith and God, the Creator and Renewer of the church." And finally, in the fourth, "The church . . . needs to be reminded of its contemporary responsibilities [and] to remember also that it is not merely contemporary; 'faithful people of all ages' constitute the church; Christians . . . recognize their unity in Christ as they strive for reconciliation."[24]

20. Ibid., 7.
21. Ibid., 8.
22. Ibid., 20.
23. Ibid., 20–21.
24. Ibid., 81–84.

Shinn's connection between "unity in Christ" and a ministry in which we "strive for reconciliation" resonates with my purpose, which is to nurture the kind of theological reflection and critical thinking necessary to the formation of conciliar identity, fostering the ability to participate in the furtherance of the ecumenical initiatives at the local level. In order to attain that goal with any degree of proficiency we must take seriously the counsel of Kathryn Tanner:

> In order to figure out how to go on, one must, with some measure of reflective exertion, figure out the meaning of what one has been doing, why one does it and what it implies—in particular, how it hangs together (or fails to hang together) with the rest of what one believes and does. Because of their ambiguities, inconsistencies, and open-endedness, practices, in short, do not run by automatic or mechanical routine but through at least quasi-reflective or deliberate effort to figure out what to do next, how to proceed.[25]

Knowledge of Christian convictions is, on its own merit, insufficient to the formation and nurture of a conciliar identity; I recognize the importance of maintaining the bond between beliefs and practices. Dorothy Bass and Craig Dykstra state that while exploration of belief-based practices assumes "different shapes in different communities," the following dynamics prove consistent in every case and are therefore helpful to bear in mind in the development of an educational program intended to advance the formation of conciliar identity:

- Consider the practice in relation to . . . how it effects the flourishing of specific groups of people in and beyond the community.
- Inquire into its ethical dimensions. Are there obstacles that keep us from engaging in the practice in ways that are good for ourselves and others?
- Consider the ways in which different communities . . . have shaped this practice. What have Christian churches . . . done, in history and today, to sustain it?
- Reflect on how a practice enables us to participate in the activity of God's Spirit in the world.

---

25. Tanner, "Theological Reflection," 232.

- Be concrete. How do people draw one another into a practice, and how do they learn it from and teach it to one another?

- Worship together, and see whether you can find the practice crystallized in the liturgy.

- Practice together—not after you have studied and talked but at the same time.[26]

Beliefs, formalized as theological interpretations, creedal affirmations, or statements of faith, are intended to shape perceptions, hopes, values—promoting a particular worldview and shaping the identity and life of the believer as well. The vision-and-vocation of the UCC, and the formation of conciliar identity expressed through practices characteristic of that same identity configuration, are vital to strengthening the identity of the local congregation as a conciliar fellowship.

The unity of the Church catholic, the reality of reconciliation, and the formation of Christian identity are fundamentally the work of God's Holy Spirit and cannot be orchestrated through an adequate pedagogy and program of education.[27] Nevertheless, I believe an educational program could be developed[28] to serve as a vehicle through which the Spirit of God can work a transformation of identity. The identity I would seek to promote is to be formed within a particular community of faith, yet the implications of that identity are wide ranging—broader and more extensive than the boundaries of the community in which the formation takes place.[29]

While the formation of conciliar identity is dependent upon sustained engagement with such an educational program, it also requires the capacity to make the connection between the ecumenical prin-

---

26. Bass and Dykstra, "Practices of Faith," 199–200.

27. Polkinghorne and Welker write: "[The apostle Paul] repeatedly describes a process of growth if those who let themselves be grasped through the Spirit." Polkinghorne and Welker, *Faith in the Living God*, 95.

28. I am in the process of revising one such educational program that I developed and employed for a short period of time to test the doctoral thesis of developing a "conciliar identity" within the local congregation. Depending on the reception the current work receives, I would hope to have the program available for publication in 2011.

29. Thomas Groome asserts: "Education ministry" must be "a deliberate and structured attempt to influence how" church members live their lives "in society. Education . . . must address us in a historical community and attempt to influence us in the way to live our time in community." Groome, *Christian Religious Education*, 15.

ciples being examined and the practices implied in those principles. In its own form my approach is similar to Paul Tillich's "method of correlation." Where I differ from Tillich's methodology is in the substance of the scheme. Tillich's "method of correlation" moves from the questions implied in human existence to the answers provided in the gospel message. My approach moves from the questions implicit in the prevailing *disunity* of the church to the implied answers provided by the *ecumenical* principles located in the resources of both the UCC vision-and-vocation and the wider ecumenical movement. Like Tillich's method, the results must be evident in some practical aspect of a much larger reflective process.[30]

Each participant in such an educational program must learn the skills necessary to do the interpretive work that inevitably takes place along the permeable boundary between *beliefs* and *practices*. The participant must learn the grammar of an ecumenical faith so that the educational program does more than outline the specific ecumenical convictions of the UCC and the wider church in some linear fashion. The program must be structured so that participants are challenged to internalize the "grammar" of an *ecumenical faith* while demonstrating the ability to relate each ecumenical conviction to some practical end. As Ford and Swan suggest:

> Good religious education programs are organized around a major principle to which all the information is related. Common themes appear in the common or agreed statements of the multilateral and bilateral dialogues of the past twenty-five years. For instance, an examination of the Lutheran bi-laterals in the United States indicates that the following themes important to Lutheran identity are generally important to most/all churches: (1) authority of Scripture, (2) creeds and documents, (3) ecclesiology, (4) sacraments, (5) ministry, (6) Gospel, and (7) justification and sanctification. These themes are important to Lutherans, but the dialogue process revealed that they were significant for the other dialogue partners, although each had a somewhat different way of stating their significance.[31]

Those who gain a deeper appreciation for the richness and value of the traditions found in the historical realities and present manifestations

---

30. For an analysis of the value of Paul Tillich's method of correlation to the development of a pedagogy suited to the education of adults in the church, see Krych, *Teaching the Gospel Today*, 25–31.

31. Ford and Swan, *Twelve Tales Untold*, 10.

of the Church catholic should also gain the capacity to articulate the ecumenical convictions of the UCC's vision-and-vocation, while demonstrating the formation of conciliar identity in process, having an advantage over those who lack this same capacity. They hold an even greater advantage over those for whom the church has become little more than a political platform or what is worse, a center for entertainment. This is not to advocate some form of pride among those who seek to attain conciliar identity; it is rather the desire to place responsibility for the furtherance of visible unity on the shoulders of those in the local congregation of the UCC, providing such members with the opportunity to embrace the very real and challenging work of ecumenicity among those brothers and sisters in Christ who are family, friend, or neighbor to them.

10

The Contributions of L. Gregory Jones and George Lindbeck

L. GREGORY JONES CRITIQUES mainline churches in North America for their failure to maintain the necessary practice of "catechesis," more broadly understood as education in the essential beliefs of the Christian tradition. He contends that this void has led to the current situation in which "the fabric of the churches is rending." He also argues that mainline churches have an awareness of the need for "more extensive catechesis as the dominant culture has become less overtly supportive of religious beliefs, desires, and practices," and yet "most congregations have failed either to sustain the structure that once nurtured Christian faith ... or to develop rich alternative methods."[1]

Jones discusses catechesis as both the primary vehicle for the full initiation of converts and as a reformative exercise for those who have been members of the church for years or for a lifetime; more than a refresher course, the use of catechesis in this way assures the maintenance of Christian identity. Looking back to the ancient practice of catechesis, the implied understanding in its use was "the conviction that the Christian life involves an ongoing journey of conversion, a process of embracing a Christian way of life." Rather than rely on a denominational institution or ministry to provide adequate education in ecumenicity, Jones contends that local churches "ought to be the settings of catechesis in which" conciliar identity is shaped "by faithful instruction and inquiry, prayer and worship, and other corporate practices that are constitutive" of the church's ecumenical life.[2]

---

1. Jones, "Theological Education," 191–94.
2. Ibid., 202.

Another dynamic in the formation of conciliar identity is found in the writing of George Lindbeck with his "cultural-linguistic" model. Learning the grammar of an ecumenical faith is, in a primary way, based on Lindbeck's use of the term. Lindbeck's argument advances along three interconnected lines of reasoning: (1) what he refers to as a "cultural-linguistic" view of religious belief and practice; (2) a "rule theory" assessment of doctrine, considered advantageous to ecumenists; and (3) an "intratextual" hermeneutic, essential to the Christian church's survival in an environment awash in pluralism and the adverse affects of modernity. Lindbeck also believes that the contemporary church is experiencing "the awkwardly intermediate stage of having once been culturally established but . . . not yet clearly disestablished."[3]

One result the church finding itself so situated is the threatened loss of Christian identity and sense of connectedness to a historically communicated confessional heritage, both of obvious concern to the ecumenical effort. A second consequence is the church's attempt to maintain relevance either by accommodation to the surrounding culture (an accusation often leveled against the UCC by her more conservative detractors) or by a theological defensiveness that borders on promoting a ghetto mentality (an accusation often leveled against the conservative detractors by those in the UCC who are said to be more "liberal").

What troubles Lindbeck most about the current cultural climate should be of equal concern to ecumenists: indifference toward the Christian community. The church is perceived to be impotent and therefore unable to assert real influence on the surrounding culture— influence consonant with the values and convictions assigned to the Christian gospel. Cultural indifference is augmented by a growing acceptance of a relativistic view of religious belief and practice, a relativism that has had an impact on ecumenical efforts as well.[4] Lindbeck argues that

> as we move into a culturally . . . post-Christian period . . . increasing numbers of people regard all religions as possible sources of symbols to be used eclectically in articulating, clarifying, and organizing the experiences of the inner self. Religions are seen

---

3. Lindbeck, *Nature of Doctrine*, 134.
4. Kinnamon, *Vision of the Ecumenical Movement*, esp. 109–119.

as multiple suppliers of different forms of a single commodity needed for transcendent self-expression and self-realization.[5]

With the increased promotion and acceptance of pluralism and relativism, "fewer and fewer contemporary people are deeply embedded in particular religious traditions or thoroughly involved in particular religious communities."[6] This has become a fertile field for the "experiential-expressive" approach to religious belief and practice, and "the rationale suggested, though not necessitated, by an experiential-expressive approach is that the various religions are diverse symbolizations of one and the same core experience of the Ultimate, and that therefore they must respect each other, learn from each other, and reciprocally enrich each other."[7] At first blush and to the degree that this situation would appear to encourage openness to dialog with those of differing traditions, it would seem a favorable environment for promotion and furtherance of the ecumenical agenda. However, the ecumenical agenda does not advocate the form of relativism implicitly (and often explicitly!) endorsed by the experiential-expressive mode of tolerance and reciprocity.

Even the most unscientific survey of many congregations in the UCC would demonstrate the veracity of Lindbeck's comment. The experiential-expressive approach to belief and practice within the UCC, indicative of a more "liberal agenda," seems to have achieved dominance, at least at the national level. This focus is also related to a softening of the church's ecumenical thrust. We should learn to "resist the claims of the religiously interested public for what is currently fashionable," while at the same time making a "greater Christian authenticity communally possible."[8]

Continuing his study of the different approaches to religious belief and practice, Lindbeck discusses the "cognitive-propositional" approach. While the experiential-expressive approach tends to be individualistic, subjective, and internally authorized (it is true only if it is true for me!), the "cognitive-propositional" approach holds that

> church doctrines are communally authoritative teachings regarding beliefs and practices that are considered essential to

---

5. Lindbeck, *Nature of Doctrine*, 22.
6. Ibid., 21.
7. Ibid., 23.
8. Ibid., 134.

the identity and welfare of the group in question. They may be formally operative, but in any case they indicate what constitutes faithful adherence to a community. A religious body cannot exist as a recognizably distinctive collectivity unless it has some beliefs and/or practices by which it can be identified.[9]

As examples Lindbeck cites the "Protestant *biblicistic* and the Catholic *traditionalist*" approaches, where identity is preserved by "reproducing as literalistically as possible the words and actions of the past."[10] It could reasonably be argued that the perennial power struggle in the UCC is between those who would favor the experiential-expressive mode and those who favor, the cognitive-propositional approach and therefore practice their faith from within its perceived security. What has not yet been adequately explored as a viable alternative, and in particular in reference to the UCC's ecumenical vision-and-vocation, is the formation of conciliar identity grounded in Lindbeck's "cultural-linguistic" approach and attending "rule theory" and "intratextual" hermeneutic.

Lindbeck himself is apparently driven by the desire to achieve several related objectives through his study and recommendations, among them is one that runs along two parallel tracks: (1) the sustainable usefulness of the distinctive Christian faith tradition in a contemporary milieu that seeks to promote pluralism as a virtue; and (2) the effort to counteract the unfortunate consequence of modernity as a sociopolitical phenomenon to some degree responsible for the unhappy fate besetting Christianity in this present era. Modernity has created a religious environment in which communal norms have been all but replaced by personal preference. As Lindbeck assesses the situation:

> The modern mood is antipathetic to the very notion of communal norms . . . the product of such factors as religious and ideological pluralism and social mobility. When human beings are insistently exposed to conflicting and changing views, they tend to lose their confidence in any one of them. Doctrines no longer represent objective realities and are instead experienced as expressions of personal preference.[11]

Under the present conditions, the church will face opposition to any attempt to establish standards of belief and practice, the effort will

9. Ibid., 74.
10. Ibid., 79.
11. Ibid., 77.

be experienced as "an intolerable infringement of the liberty of the self." The experiential-expressive approach is then "used to legitimate the religious privatism and subjectivism that is fostered by the social pressure of the day."[12]

The "liberal agenda"—theologically speaking—has sought to discover a universal principle capable of serving as an acceptable foundation for Christian beliefs. Advocates of a "postliberal" agenda (e.g., Lindbeck) remain less than convinced, skeptical of the merit in seeking a foundation in principles external to the church's own biblically and historically shaped theological tradition. The postliberal agenda seeks to provide the church an opportunity to reinvigorate its own unique identity amid the pluralism of contemporary culture. Supporting those who advocate that the church undertake the problem of identity, Lindbeck recommends that the church do so by remaining faithful to its own traditional cultural-linguistic particularities.[13]

The cultural-linguistic approach (the method of "postliberals") locates religious meaning within the text of the faith-community and the symbols generated by the hermeneutical exchange between the text, community, and world in their interactions. Meaning is inherently derived from the way in which a particular language is used in a given tradition. Lindbeck claims that meaning is constituted by the uses of a specific language rather than being distinguishable from it. Thus the proper way to determine what "God" signifies, for example, is by examining how the word operates within a religion, and thereby shapes reality and experience rather than by first establishing its propositional or experiential meaning and reinterpreting or reforming its use accordingly. The cultural-linguistic approach downplays the cognitive dimension of religious belief; of primary importance is "the conceptual vocalizing and syntax—or inner logic which determines the kinds of truth claims the religion can make." Religion is not a deliberate choice to adhere to fixed propositions, rather, to become religious one must "interiorize a set of skills by practice and training." For my purposes this would mean learning to think, reason, and act in a way that conforms to the "intratextual" features of the ecumenical vision-and-vocation of the UCC: "the cultural-linguistic model is part of an outlook that stresses the degree to

12. Ibid.
13. Ibid., 130–32.

which ... to become religious involves becoming skilled in the language, the symbol system of a given religion."[14]

Religious language functions like any other formal grammar and is guided by particular "rules" of usage. Referring to rules in a more general way, Lindbeck argues that "oppositions between rules can in some instances be resolved, not by altering one or both of them, but by specifying when or where they apply, or by stipulating which of the competing doctrines takes precedence." Christian doctrine "regulates truth claims by excluding some and permitting others." Tracing this concept back into the theological and historical uses of doctrine, Lindbeck avers that the "notion of *regulae fidei* goes back to the earliest Christian centuries, and later historians and systematic theologians have often recognized in varying degrees that the operational logic of religious teachings in their communally authoritative role is regulative."[15]

On the question of practicality, Lindbeck argues that "religious communities are likely to be practically relevant in the long run to the degree that they do not first ask what is either practical or relevant, but instead concentrate on their own intratextual outlooks and forms of life." This also implies that "the grammar of religion, like that of language, cannot be explicated or learned by analysis or experience, but only in their own terms, not by transposing them into alien speech." Generally speaking, "religions are seen as comprehensive interpretive schemes, usually embodied in myths or narratives and heavily ritualized, which structure human experience and understanding of the self and world."[16]

LINDBECK'S IMPLIED ECUMENICITY

Throughout his work, Lindbeck displays a deep sensitivity to the issues raised for the Christian in a pluralistic environment and does so in a way that is neither contentious nor supercilious. Addressing the Christian claim to the unparalleled revelation of God in Christ (a claim to exclusivity) as the foundation for a "language" that can speak with unequaled authority, Lindbeck writes:

> To hold that a particular language is the only one that has the words and the concepts that can authentically speak of the

---

14. Ibid., 114, 38, 18, respectively.
15. Ibid., 19, 128, respectively.
16. Ibid., 129, 32, 61, respectively.

ground of being, the goal of history, and true humanity (for Christians believe they cannot genuinely speak of these apart from telling the biblical story) is not at all the same as denying that other religions have resources for speaking truths and referring to realities, even highly important truths and realities, of which Christianity as yet knows nothing and by which it could be greatly enriched.[17]

This perspective eventuates in a description of the church's evangelistic effort that would not win the approval of some, even in ecumenical circles, but it is commendable for the way in which it resonates with the conciliatory approach of the vision-and-vocation of the UCC: "The communication of the gospel is not a form of psychotherapy, but rather the offer and act of sharing one's beloved language—the language that speaks of Jesus Christ—with all those who are interested, in full awareness that God does not call all to be part of the witnessing people."[18]

Lindbeck also asserts that while some doctrines are "conditional," others are clearly intended to be "unconditional." *Unconditional* doctrines are "part of the indispensable grammar or logic of the faith," for example, there are "no circumstances in which Christians are commanded not to love God or neighbor." Other doctrines are conditionally essential, yet "while all unconditionally essential doctrines are permanent, the *conditional* variety may be either permanent or temporary."

In an effort to clarify the distinction, Lindbeck states that "whenever such and such a condition prevails, such and such a doctrine applies. It is this condition, not the doctrine, which is temporary or 'reformable.'"[19] Illustrating his point with a reference to church history, Lindbeck writes that "from the very beginning" Christianity has been "committed to the possibility of expressing the same faith, the same teaching, and the same doctrine in diverse ways." As an example, he points to "the multiplicity of Christological titles in the New Testament" where no "particular words or specific interpretive notions are uniquely sacrosanct."[20] One could also return to the affirmation of Vincent of Lerins ("that which has been believed everywhere, always, and by all") not so much as a manifestation of inflexibility as it is an assertion that one be clear in the

17. Ibid.
18. Ibid., 85.
19. Ibid., 87.
20. Ibid., 92.

distinction between what is "unconditional" and "conditional" in matters of doctrine and tradition.

SUMMATION

The promise of Lindbeck's project is beyond question. Not only is his theoretical model differentiating between experiential-expressive, cognitive-propositional, and cultural-linguistic approaches to religious beliefs and practices insightful, his conceptual framework of both "rule theory" and "intratextuality" in doctrinal explication helps clarify the distinction between strictly defined denominational configurations and those of a wider ecumenical interest, representative of the Church catholic. Experiential-expressive and cognitive-propositional approaches have been tried and found wanting. The cultural-linguistic approach holds great promise as a theoretical model advancing the renewal of the UCC's ecumenical vision-and-vocation. Moreover, the cultural-linguistic approach seems most congenial to ecumenicity and the characteristics of a genuinely informed conciliar identity.

More specifically, while the UCC lays claim to being a *united* and *uniting* church, the historical realities of this young church demonstrate that claim to be, at best, incongruous. Even if hyperbolic, I contend that there has been and continues to be a historical polarity between experiential-expressivists and cognitive-propositionalists spread throughout the UCC. Lindbeck's project provides a theoretical model with which to analyze the deeper dynamics of our divisions, recommending a helpful alternative for the restoration of harmony and the advance of ecumenicity throughout the church.

While there is much in George Lindbeck's work that is open to debate, his description of the cultural-linguistic approach to belief and practice serves as a catalyst for the development of an alternative comprehension of what it means to belong to a conciliar fellowship, consistent in its claim to seek ever more visible expressions of our unity in Christ. After all, with such focus the local congregation is better equipped to give primacy to the proper object of faith—a Person rather than a set of propositions. Lindbeck's model provides a kind of prophetic admonition that all members of the UCC would do well to heed. Without some clear measure of consensus on what it means to be a conciliar Christian, or what truly constitutes the church's vision-and-vocation, there can be no meaningful context within which dialogue can continue and the hope of ecumenical interests be realized.

In conclusion, I leave the reader with the words of Dietrich Bonhoeffer (we began, and it is only fitting we end, with him!) from a sermon preached in 1933, based on the Gospel text of Matthew (16:13–18):

> No human being builds the church, but Christ alone. Anyone who proposes to build the church is certainly already on the way to destroying it, because it will turn out to be a temple of idolatry, though the builder does not intend that or know it. We are to confess, while God builds. We are to preach, while God builds. We are to pray, while God builds. . . . It is a great comfort that Christ gives to the church: "You confess, preach, bear witness to me, but I alone will do the building, wherever I am pleased to do so. . . . Don't look for anyone's opinion; don't ask them what they think. Don't keep calculating; don't look around for support from others. Not only must church remain church, but you, my church, confess, confess, confess." . . . Christ alone is your Lord; by his grace alone you live, just as you are. Christ is building.[21]

---

21. Bonhoeffer, *Berlin: 1932–1933*, 480–81.

11

Postscript

ON MORE THAN ONE occasion throughout this work I have quoted from a book titled *The Church: Readings in Theology*; the following is taken from an essay authored by Hugo Rahner, in which he quotes Pius XII from his encyclical titled *Mystici Corporis*:

> Probably there is much in the Church that betrays the weakness of our human nature. Her divine founder, however, endures these weaknesses. He endures them even in the higher members of his mystical body, for this reason, so that in this way the strength of the virtuousness of the flock and the shepherds will be tested, and that the merits of faith should grow in each of them. Christ would wish to know that even sinners are not shut out of this community. Therefore, the fact that many members suffer from spiritual infirmity is no reason for us to lessen our love for the Church, rather it is an occasion for us to feel deeper sympathy with her members.[1]

Elaborating on these thoughtful words of Pius XII, Rahner makes the following staggering claim:

> We must cherish the Church as Christ does. We must fill her with warm love. We must console her and embrace her. We must intercede for her with the jealousy of God. In a word, we must love her in her totality and without conditions. And behold, precisely in this love, the transformation of the Church from weakness to power, from crippled ugliness to immortal beauty, is taking place, silently and irresistibly until the end of time. Where this love is alive the Church grows up to the healthy maturity of the Lord. Already here below she will become the victorious, the eternal, the living Church. This is the mystery of the weak Church. . . .

---

1. Rahner, "The Church, God's Strength," 13.

> This is the Church of our weakness and our strength. Flames in the desert of life, home on our wandering way, promised land already here before our happy arrival.[2]

Both statements resonate with the objective I have had in mind while researching and writing this book; for more than thirty years I have joyously endured a lover's quarrel with the *church* as I have come to know, serve, and embrace her (that is, as the *United Church of Christ*). Even so, I now believe that we face a "crisis" of identity unparalleled in the history of our being a faith community, and the time has come for decisive dialog in the development of an ecclesiology that gives evidence of our having clearly comprehended what is it for *church* to be and become *Church*!

One need not step outside the boundaries of our own antecedent traditions in order to hear the clarion call to ecumenicity, to pursue with all due devotion and dedication greater visibility to the *one, holy, catholic, and apostolic church* embodied in the originating vision-and-vocation of the UCC. Exploration of those same theological traditions will quickly disclose, and across the spectrum of history and confessional conviction, the desire to engage in ecumenical endeavors in obedience to Christ and the longing so forcefully expressed in his high-priestly prayer (John 17).

My avowed purpose is not all that different from that attributed to both Nevin and Schaff (of the Mercersburg theology) by W. Bradford Littlejohn when he asserts:

> If fidelity to Scripture and the testimony of the historic Church compelled them [i.e., Nevin and Schaff] to revise or augment a part of the Reformed tradition, they gladly did so, for to be a Christian, and in unity with the one, holy, catholic, and apostolic Church was more important than being distinctively Reformed. They knew better than to suppose Reformed theology had all the answers. . . . But in none of this did they lightly abandon their heritage, for how could they be faithful to the Church of all ages if they did not even know how to be faithful to the Church of their childhood . . . [in this] their demonstration of how to be Reformed because they were catholic, catholic because they were Reformed. . . . Nevin and Schaff have a thing or two to teach us today.[3]

---

2. Ibid., 13–14.
3. Littlejohn, *Mercersburg Theology*, 183.

Without claiming more for my own ecclesiology than would be appropriate or could reasonably be defended, I have attempted to offer one approach to the development of *an* ecclesiology that would be a more faithful, and perhaps even fruitful, representation of the intent of those who worked so hard, gave so much, and invested their own dreams and hopes in the future promise of even greater ecumenical achievements through the United Church of Christ as a *united* and *uniting* church.

Beyond that, I have come to the firm conviction that in almost every form the church has assumed in our contemporary setting (North America and Western Christianity in particular!) self-identification has had far more to do with self-preservation; in the promotion of what is said to be "uniquely" attributable to this "church" over against that "church"; we find ourselves engaged (and embattled!) in competition for "new members," even at the cost of biblical and theological integrity. There is an agenda prevalent in most churches having little or nothing to do with a faithful continuation of handing on the biblical and theological traditions that were once the bulwark of confessional truth, rather, churches have everything to do with cultural accommodation.

The reclamation of an ecumenical faith is not a task placed solely on the shoulders of UCC leaders or as a privilege of the UCC; it is rather the task to be taken up by all who claim to be "church," confessing obedience to Christ. That is why I contend that this book is not written for members of the UCC alone; none of us—Protestant, Roman Catholic, Pan-Orthodox—can simply divorce ourselves from the high and holy calling to pursue greater manifestations of visible unity. We ignore this, one of our fundamental callings in Christ, only at the risk of rejection by the world we seek to call to salvation, and the loss of a most valued mark of identification as the *one, holy, catholic, and apostolic church.* To the degree that the pursuit of visible unity becomes a line item far down on the church's list of priorities, we fail to demonstrate reconciliation and "wholeness," which come as a consequence of the glorious gospel of grace, and in fact betray that same truth by virtue of our indifference to the brokenness of Christ's body!

What I have claimed throughout this book and will continue to assert in whatever ways God makes possible is that the UCC has always had a very special calling to the pursuit of unity; the further she distances herself from that same calling, the more she will come to experience a diminution of discipleship and a loss of voice in a world wracked with divisions of every kind. We face a day of decision, and the steps we take could prove to be either a blessing to and further enrichment of those who will follow us in future generations of believers, or bring an end to what was once a faith community of such immense promise.

I choose to conclude on a *positive* rather than a *negative* note. The whole of my purpose in writing this book to the confessional community addressed throughout (that is, the United Church of Christ), and to the Church catholic in each of her splendid and varied confessional bodies, can be summarized in the words of Paul Claudel. Acknowledging that the following is an affirmation of the catholicity of our beloved church in her form as Roman Catholic confession, can we not hope and pray that these same words one day—and soon—will become both confession and reality for the United Church of Christ in the reclamation of her vision-and-vocation as a *united* and *uniting* church?

> All the saints and angels belong to us. We can use the intelligence of St. Thomas, the right arm of St. Michael, the hearts of Joan of Arc and Catherine of Siena, and all the hidden resources which have only to be touched to be set in action. Everything of the good, the great and the beautiful from one end of the earth to the other—everything which *begets* sanctity (as a doctor says of a patient that he has *got* a fever)—it is as if all that were our work. The heroism of the missionary, the inspiration of the Doctors of the Church, the generosity of the martyrs, the genius of the artists, the burning prayer of the Poor Clares and Carmelites—it is as if all that were ourselves; it is ourselves. All that is one with us, from the North to the South, from the Alpha to the Omega, for the Orient to the Occident; we clothe ourselves in it.[4]

---

4. De Lubac, *Splendor of the Church*, 176.

Bibliography

Achtemeier, P. Mark. "The *Union with Christ* Doctrine in Renewal: Movements of the Presbyterian Church (USA)." In Alston and Welker, *Reformed Theology*, 336-52.
Alston, Wallace M., Jr., and Michael Welker. *Reformed Theology: Identity and Ecumenicity*. Grand Rapids, MI: Eerdmans, 2003.
Barnes, M. Craig. *Searching for Home: Spirituality for Restless Souls*. Grand Rapids, MI: Brazos, 2003.
Bass, Dorothy C. *Practicing Our Faith: A Way of Life for a Searching People*. San Francisco: Jossey-Bass, 1997.
Bass, Dorothy C., and Craig Dykstra. "Growing into the Practices of Faith." In Bass, *Practicing Our Faith*, 185-205.
Bendroth, Margaret Lamberts, Lawrence N. Jones, and Robert A. Schneider, eds. *The Living Theological Heritage of the United Church of Christ*. Vol. 5, *Outreach and Diversity*. Cleveland: Pilgrim, 2000.
Bonhoeffer, Dietrich. *Berlin: 1932-1933*. Vol. 2 of *Dietrich Bonhoeffer Works*. Edited by Larry L. Rasmussen. Translated by Isabel Best and David Higgins. Minneapolis: Fortress, 2009.
Best, Isabel, Lisa E. Dahill, Reinhard Krauss, and Nancy Lukens, eds. *Letters and Papers From Prison*. Vol. 8 of *Dietrich Bonhoeffer Works*. Translated by John W. de Gruchy. Minneapolis: Fortress, 2009.
Braaten, Carl E., and Robert W. Jenson. *In One Body through the Cross: The Princeton Proposal for Christian Unity*. Grand Rapids, MI: Eerdmans, 2003.
———. *The Ecumenical Future*. Grand Rapids, MI: Eerdmans, 2004.
Brinkman, Martien E. *Progress In Unity? Fifty Years of Theology within the World Council of Churches: 1945-1995; A Study Guide*. Louvian Theological and Pastoral Monographs 18. Grand Rapids, MI: Eerdmans and Peeters, 1995.
Brueggemann, Walter. *Covenanted Self: Explorations in Law and Covenant*. Minneapolis: Fortress, 1999.
———. *The Land : Place As Gift, Promise and Challenge in Biblical Faith*. Philadelphia: Fortress, 1977.
Busch, Eberhard. "Reformed Strength in its Denominational Weakness." In Alston and Welker, *Reformed Theology*, 20-33.
Cassidy, Edward Idris. "Ecumenical Education and Formation: An Urgent Need for Further Progress in Ecumenical and Interfaith Relations." In Cunningham, *Ecumenism*, 51-60.
Charry, Ellen T. *By the Renewing of Your Minds: The Pastoral Function of Christian Doctrine*. New York: Oxford University Press, 1997.
Cochrane, Arthur. "Karl Barth's Doctrine of the Covenant." In McKim, *Major Themes in the Reformed Tradition*, 108-116.

Bibliography

Crites, Stephen. "The Narrative Quality of Experience." In *Why Narrative? Readings in Narrative Theology*, edited by Stanley Hauerwas and L. Gregory Jones, 65–88. Grand Rapids, MI: Eerdmans, 1989.

Cunningham, Lawrence S. *Ecumenism: Present Realties and Future Prospects*. Notre Dame, IN: University of Notre Dame Press, 1998.

De Lubac, Henri. *The Splendor of the Church*. Translated by Michael Mason. New York: Sheed and Ward, 1956.

Dipko, Thomas E. Postscript to *Growing Toward Unity*. Edited by Elsabeth Slaughter Hilkke. Vol. 6 of *The Living Theological Heritage of the United Church of Christ*, edited by Barbara Brown Zikmund. Cleveland: Pilgrim, 1998.

Dykstra, Craig. *Growing in the Life of Faith: Education and Christian Practices*. Louisville: Geneva Press, 1999.

Dykstra, Craig, and Dorothy Bass. "A Theological Understanding of Practices." In Dykstra and Bass, *Practicing Theology*, 13–32.

Ford, John T., and Darlis J. Swan. *Twelve Tales Untold: A Study Guide in Ecumenical Reception*. Grand Rapids, MI: Eerdmans, 1993.

Fries, Heinrich. *Unity of the Churches: An Actual Possibility*. Translated by Eric Gritsch. Philadelphia: Fortress, 1985.

Groome, Thomas H. *Christian Religious Education: Sharing Our Story and Vision*. San Francisco: Harper & Row, 1980.

———. *Sharing Faith: A Comprehensive Approach to Religious Education and Pastoral Ministry*. New York: HarperCollins, 1991.

Gros, Jeffrey, Eamon McManus, and Ann Riggs. *Introduction to Ecumenism*. New York: Paulist Press, 1998.

Gros, Jeffrey, Harding Meyer, and William Rusch. *Growth in Agreement II: Reports and Agreed Statements of Ecumenical Conversations on a World Level, 1982–1998*. Geneva: WCC / Eerdmans, 2000.

Guardini, Romano. "The Church: Encounter with Christ." In LaPierre, Verkamp, Wetterer, and Zeitler, *The Church: Readings in Theology*, 19–29.

Guder, Darrell L. *The Continuing Conversion of the Church*. Grand Rapids, MI: Eerdmans, 2000.

Gunnemann, Louis H. *The Shaping of the United Church of Christ: An Essay in the History of American Christianity*. Expanded by Charles Shelby Rooks. Cleveland: United Church Press, 1999.

———. *United and Uniting: The Meaning of an Ecclesial Journey; United Church of Christ 1957–1987*. Cleveland: United Church Press, 1987.

Hall, Douglas John. *Confessing the Faith: Christian Theology in a North American Context*. Minneapolis: Augsburg Fortress, 1996.

———. *Professing the Faith: Christian Theology in a North American Context*. Minneapolis: Augsburg Fortress, 1993.

———. *Thinking the Faith: Christian Theology in a North American Context*. Minneapolis: Augsburg Fortress, 1989.

Hambrick-Stowe, Charles, ed. *Colonial and National Beginnings*. Vol. 3 of *The Living Theological Heritage of the United Church of Christ*, edited by Barbara Brown Zikmund. Cleveland: Pilgrim, 1998.

Hilke, Elsabeth Slaughter, ed. *Growing Toward Unity*. Postscript by Thomas E. Dipko. Vol. 6 of *The Living Theological Heritage of the United Church of Christ*, edited by Barbara Brown Zikmund. Cleveland: Pilgrim, 1998.

Jones, Serene. "Graced Practices: Excellence and Freedom in the Christian Life." In Volf and Bass, *Practicing Theology*, 55–71.

Jones, L. Gregory. "Beliefs, Desires, Practices, and the Ends of Theological Education." In Volf and Bass, *Practicing Theology*, 185–205.
Jungmann, Josef. "The Holy Church." In LaPierre, Verkamp, Wetterer, and Zeitler, *The Church: Readings in Theology*, 30–39.
Kinnamon, Michael. *The Vision of the Ecumenical Movement and How It Has Been Impoverished by Its Friends*. St. Louis: Chalice, 2003.
Kinnamon, Michael, and Brian E. Cope. *The Ecumenical Movement: An Anthology of Key Texts and Voices*. Geneva: WCC / Eerdmans, 1997.
Klempa, William. "The Concept of the Covenant in Sixteenth- and Seventeenth-Century Continental and British Reformed Theology." In McKim, *Major Themes in Reformed Tradition*, 95–107.
Körtner, Ulrich. "Paradox Catholicity: The Union of Identity and Difference as a Core Problem of Christian Ecumenicity." In Alston and Welker, *Reformed Theology*, 398–411.
Krych, Margaret. *Teaching the Gospel Today: A Guide to Education in the Congregation*. Minneapolis: Augsburg, 1981.
Lambert, Bernard. *Ecumenism: Theology and History*. New York: Herder and Herder, 1967.
LaPierre, Albert, Bernard Verkamp, Edward Wetterer, and John Zeitler, eds. *The Church: Readings in Theology*. New York: Kenedy, 1963.
Lerins, Vincent of. "Commonitories." *The Fathers of the Church*, vol. 7. Translated by Rudolph E. Morris. New York: Fathers of the Church, 1949.
Lindbeck, George A. *The Church in a Postliberal Age*. Edited by James J. Buckely. Grand Rapids, MI: Eerdmans, 2002.
———. *The Nature of Doctrine: Religion and Theology in a Postliberal Age*. Philadelphia: Westminster, 1984.
Littlejohn, W. Bradford. *The Mercersburg Theology and the Quest for Reformed Catholicity*. Eugene, OR: Pickwick Publications, 2009.
McKim, Donald K., ed. *Major Themes in Reformed Theology*. Grand Rapids, MI: Eerdmans, 1992.
Meyer, Harding. *That All May Be One: Perceptions and Models of Ecumenicity*. Translated by William G. Rusch. Grand Rapids, MI: Eerdmans, 1999.
Migliore, Daniel. "The Communion of the Triune God: Towards a Trinitarian Ecclesiology in Reformed Perspective." In Alston and Welker, *Reformed Theology*, 140–54.
Naudé, Piet J. "Identity and Ecumenicity: How Do We Deal Theologically with So-Called 'Nontheological' Factors?" In Alston and Welker, *Reformed Theology*, 435–49.
Newbigin, Lesslie. *The Gospel in a Pluralist Society*. London: SPCK, 1997.
———. "What Is 'a Local Church Truly United'?" In Kinnamon, *The Ecumenical Movement*, 114–120.
Niebuhr, H. Richard. *The Social Sources of Denominationalism*. Cleveland: World Publishing, 1957.
Nordbeck, Elizabeth C., and Lowell H. Zuck, eds. *Consolidation and Expansion*. Vol. 4 of *The Living Theological Heritage of the United Church of Christ*, edited by Barbara Brown Zikmund. Cleveland: Pilgrim, 1999.
Nygren, Anders. *Christ and His Church*. Translated by Alan Carlsten. Philadelphia: Westminster Press, 1956.
Paul, Robert S. *Freedom with Order: The Doctrine of the Church in the United Church of Christ*. Cleveland: United Church Press, 1987.
Pauw, Amy Plantinga. "Attending the Gaps between Beliefs and Practices." In Volf and Bass, *Practicing Theology*, 33–48.

Payne, John B., ed. *Reformation Roots*. Vol. 2 of *The Living Theological Heritage of the United Church of Christ*, edited by Barbara Brown Zikmund. Cleveland: Pilgrim, 1997.

Polkinghorne, John, and Michael Welker. *Faith in the Living God: A Dialogue*. London: SPCK, 2001.

Porter, "Gathered for Life: Official Report, Sixth Assembly, World Council of Churches." In Kinnamon, *The Ecumenical Movement*, 52–61.

Radner, Ephraim. *The End of the Church: A Pneumatology of Christian Division in the West*. Grand Rapids, MI: Eerdmans, 1998.

Rahner, Hugo. "The Church, God's Strength." In LaPierre, Verkamp, Wetterer, and Zeitler, *The Church: Readings in Theology*, 257–80.

Raiser, Konrad. "Laity in the Ecumenical Movement." *TER* 45 (1993) 372–75.

———. *To Be the Church: Challenges and Hopes for a New Millennium*. Geneva: WCC, 1997.

Reno, R. R. *In the Ruins of the Church: Sustaining Faith in an Age of Diminished Christianity*. Grand Rapids, MI: Brazos, 2002.

Robinson, Anthony B. *Transforming Congregational Culture*. Grand Rapids, MI: Eerdmans, 2003.

Sell, Alan P. F. *A Reformed, Evangelical, Catholic Theology: The Contribution of the World Alliance of Reformed Churches, 1875–1982*. Eugene, OR: Wipf and Stock, 1998.

Sheldrake, Philip. *Spaces for the Sacred: Place, Memory and Identity; The Hulsean Lectures 2001*. London: SCM, 2001.

Shinn, Roger L. *Confessing Our Faith: An Interpretation of the Statement of Faith of the United Church of Christ*. Cleveland: United Church Press, 1990.

———. *Unity and Diversity in the United Church of Christ*. Royal Oak, MI: Cathedral Publishers, 1972.

Stringfellow, William. *A Public and Private Faith*. Grand Rapids, MI: Eerdmans, 1962.

Stroup, "Reformed Identity in an Ecumenical World." In Alston and Welker, *Reformed Theology*, 257–70.

Tanner, Kathryn. "Theological Reflection and Christian Practice." In Volf and Bass, *Practicing Theology*, 228–42.

Thomas, John H. "Salt That Seasons: Ecclesial Traditions in an Ecumenical Age," Kantonen Lectures, October 18, 2000.

Ulrich, Reinhold. *Ancient and Medieval Legacies*. Vol. 1 of *The Living Theological Heritage of the United Church of Christ*, edited by Barbara Brown Zikmund. Cleveland: Pilgrim, 1995.

Volf, Miroslav, and Dorothy C. Bass, editors. *Practicing Theology: Beliefs and Practices in Christian Life*. Grand Rapids, MI: Eerdmans, 2002.

Walsh, Albert. "One Model of Christian Identity: The Promise of Mercersburg Theology in the Formation of and Ecumenical Identity Unique to the United Church of Christ." In *Prism: A Theological Forum of the United Church of Christ*, edited by Clyde J. Steckel and Elizabeth C. Nordbeck, 17, no. 2 (2002) 50–62.

Weinrich, Michael. "The Openness and Worldliness of the Church." In Alston and Welker, *Reformed Theology*, 412–434.

Willard, Dallas. *The Divine Conspiracy: Rediscovering Our Hidden Life in God*. San Francisco: HarperSanFrancisco, 1998.

Zikmund, Barbara Brown, ed. *The Living Theological Heritage of the United Church of Christ*. 6 vols. Cleveland: Pilgrim, 1995–2001.

www.ingramcontent.com/pod-product-compliance
Lightning Source LLC
Chambersburg PA
CBHW070943160426
43193CB00011B/1798